Exeter
Branch

Date Due

C_____ born
Lo_____ Churc
O: _____ Natior
Se_____ 'Maril
M_____ ence
de_____ shed
ac_____ He then
be_____ nanager
on_____ urt and
ac_____ espeare
Me_____ s. From
the_____ ced and
dir_____ ing *The
Ro_____ the New
Sc_____ er *Son*,
apl_____

Fro_____ ondon.

'Ex_____ docu-
me_____ *Sunday*
'O_____ ead ...
Th_____ urotics'
_____ *y Times*

'Th_____ an this,
but_____ *elegraph*

Fruity, lascivious, apple-cart upturning ... quite wondrously
and toe-curlingly frank ... packed with the tastiest little nuggets
of gossip'
                                                          The Times

'Sheer delight .. a diarist who is
as his older brother Alan'
                    CHARL__

'The funniest account of life in
studio known to me'

'My favourite book of the year'   JOAN COLLINS

By the same author

The Prince, the Showgirl and Me
Younger Brother, Younger Son: A Memoir

My Week with Marilyn

Colin Clark

HarperCollins*Publishers*

HarperCollins*Publishers*
77–85 Fulham Palace Road,
Hammersmith, London w6 8jb

The HarperCollins website address is:
www.**fire**and**water**.com

This paperback edition 2001
1 3 5 7 9 8 6 4 2

First published in Great Britain
by HarperCollins*Publishers* 2000

Copyright © Colin Clark 2000

Colin Clark asserts the moral right to be
identified as the author of this work

ISBN 0 00 653179 2

Set in New Baskerville

Printed and bound in Great Britain by
Omnia Books Limited, Glasgow

For Christopher

CONTENTS

ILLUSTRATIONS

Marilyn photographed by Jack Cardiff in 1956, shortly
  after the events described in this book. © *Jack Cardiff*
Two photographs taken of Marilyn at Parkside House by
  Jack Cardiff. © *Jack Cardiff*
Marilyn at the London first night of Arthur Miller's *A
  View from the Bridge*. © *Hulton Getty*
Marilyn with Olivier on the set of *The Prince and the
  Showgirl*. © *1999 Archives of Milton Greene, LLC. All
  Rights Reserved. www.archivesmhg.com*
I was given the job of third assistant director on *The
  Prince and the Showgirl* because my parents were friends
  of Laurence Olivier.
Milton Greene. © *1999 Archives of Milton Greene, LLC. All
  Rights Reserved. www.archivesmhg.com*
Marilyn photographed by Jack Cardiff. © *Jack Cardiff*
Marilyn on the lot for the coronation scene, being
  attended to by hairdresser Gordon Bond, under the
  eye of Jack Cardiff. © *1999 Archives of Milton Greene,
  LLC. All Rights Reserved. www.archivesmhg.com*
Olivier trying to teach Jeremy Spenser to slide down the

banister. © *1999 Archives of Milton Greene, LLC. All Rights Reserved. www.archivesmhg.com*

Marilyn poses a problem. © *1999 Archives of Milton Greene, LLC. All Rights Reserved. www.archivesmhg.com*

Marilyn as Elsie Marina with her friend Fanny, played by Daphne Anderson. © *1999 Archives of Milton Greene, LLC. All Rights Reserved. www.archivesmhg.com*

INTRODUCTION

All my life I have kept diaries, but this is not one of them. This is a fairy story, an interlude, an episode outside time and space which nevertheless was real. And why not? I believe in magic. My life and most people's lives are a series of little miracles – strange coincidences which spring from uncontrollable impulses and give rise to incomprehensible dreams. We spend a lot of time pretending that we are normal, but underneath the surface each one of us knows that he or she is unique.

This book sets out to describe a miracle – a few days in my life when a dream came true and my only talent was not to close my eyes. Of course I didn't realise quite what a miracle it was at the time. I had been brought up in a world of 'make believe'. My earliest memory of my parents is of remote and wonderful beings, only seen late at night, wearing full evening dress. All their friends seemed to be exotic too. Actors, artists, ballerinas and opera singers filled our house with a wonderful feeling of excitement and unreality.

And there was my older brother, Alan. Alan's imagination knew no bounds, even then. My twin sister and I were

completely under his spell, and he led us into a succession
of fantastical adventures and games. It was hardly surprising
that by the age of twelve I had decided that 'show business'
would one day be the life for me; and so it has been ever
since.

I got my first job in the summer of 1956, at the age of
twenty-three, working on a film called *The Sleeping Prince*,
starring Laurence Olivier and Marilyn Monroe. I had just
come down from university, and I had no experience whatever. I was only employed because my parents were friends
of Olivier and his wife, Vivien Leigh. The Oliviers had been
frequent visitors to our home, Saltwood Castle in Kent, and
they had become part of my extended family.

The news that Olivier, the best-known classical actor of
his generation, was going to make a film with Marilyn Monroe, the famous Hollywood film star, caused a sensation.
Marilyn was to play the part which had been taken by Vivien
herself in the play by Terence Rattigan on which the film
was based. Up to then she had only played strippers and
chorus girls, in very limited roles. In 1955, after a terrific
struggle, she renegotiated her contract with Twentieth
Century-Fox and announced her intention to do more serious work. Typecasting is never easy to escape, especially in
films. Her first new role had been that of a stripper (in *Bus
Stop*), and the second, chosen for her by Milton Greene,
her partner in the newly formed Marilyn Monroe Productions, was that of a chorus girl. The only 'serious'
element was that both films were by so-called 'serious'
writers. *Bus Stop* had been based on a play by William Inge,
and *The Sleeping Prince* on a play by Terence Rattigan.

Filming *The Prince and the Showgirl*, as it was finally called (it was decided that the title should include a reference to Marilyn's character), went badly from the very beginning. Olivier patronised Monroe and treated her like a dumb blonde. This was exactly what she was trying to escape, and she resented it intensely. It also drastically affected her self-confidence, and as a result she constantly relied for advice on her 'dramatic coach', Paula Strasberg, whom Olivier distrusted. Paula's husband Lee Strasberg, the head of the Actors' Studio in New York, was trying to control Monroe from across the Atlantic. At the same time he was extracting a huge salary for his wife, which made him very unpopular. Monroe's new husband, the playwright Arthur Miller, was treating her like a difficult child, and this also undermined her. Milton Greene was desperate to retain control of 'his' star, and was letting her take more prescription drugs than was perhaps wise. But Monroe was determined to show that she could act, despite her feelings of inadequacy when faced with Olivier and the super-professional English team that had been assembled specially for the film.

From my first day on the production as third assistant director – the lowest of the low – I kept a journal of everything that I observed. I intended to transcribe it when the film was over, but my notes became messy and hard to read, and I simply put the volume away and forgot it. Forty years later I dug it out and read it again, and it was subsequently published under the title *The Prince, the Showgirl and Me.*

One episode, however, was not recorded in my diary.

For nine days in the middle of filming, I made no entries

at all. Suddenly, and completely unexpectedly, something happened which was, to me, so dramatic and so extraordinary that it was impossible to include it in my daily chatterings. For a short time the attention of the major participants – Olivier, Greene and, above all, Marilyn – seemed to be focused on me. It was as if a spotlight had swung round, for no particular reason, and singled me out as the hero or villain of the piece.

When normal life resumed, I continued to write my diary as before. I made notes on what I felt had been the key events of those 'missing' days, but that is all. It was not until the filming was over that I could go back and write down what had happened, in the form of a letter to the friend for whom I was keeping my journal.

This, then, is the story of those missing nine days. Of course it goes much further than the letter (the text of which is reproduced as an appendix to this book), but I make no apology for that. The whole episode is still as fresh in my mind as if it had happened yesterday.

I could never have written this account while Marilyn was alive. I produce it now as a humble tribute to someone who changed my life, and whose own life I only wish I could have saved.

1956

'Can't Roger handle it?' asked Milton Greene.

Milton and I were pacing up and down the small piece of new lawn outside Marilyn Monroe's dressing room at Pinewood Studios. As usual, Milton could not make up his mind.

'I'm not sure if anyone from the film crew should go near her home, Colin. Even you.'

'I rented that house for Marilyn, just as I rented yours for you,' I said. 'I hired Roger as her bodyguard, and I also hired her cook, her butler and her chauffeur. I know them all well. If we aren't very careful, everyone will just walk out. Roger is a very nice man, but Roger is a policeman. He's only used to dealing with subordinates. You can't treat servants like that. You have to behave as if they were part of the family. Believe me, Milton, I'm very familiar with these problems. My mother worries more about her cook than she does about me.'

Milton groaned. He had gone to great lengths – and considerable personal expense, he told me – to make absolutely sure that Marilyn was happy in every way. A sumptuous dressing-room suite had been built in the old make-up block at Pinewood, all beige and white, and I had taken a lease on the most beautiful house I could find – Parkside House at Englefield Green, a few miles away, which belonged to Garrett and Joan Moore, old friends of my parents. Despite all this, Marilyn did not seem to be satisfied, and Milton's pacing was distinctly uneasy.

'OK, Colin, go over to the house if you must. We can't have the servants leave. Marilyn would be mad. But whatever you do, don't let her see you. You are Sir Laurence's personal assistant, after all. And she definitely doesn't seem too keen on Sir Laurence these days.'

That was certainly true. After only three weeks of filming, a gulf had already opened between the two great stars, and everyone had started to take sides. The entire British film crew had been selected by Olivier to give him maximum support. Marilyn had brought only a small team from Hollywood – including her make-up man and her hair stylist – and they had all gone back by now. She was left with no one to support her in the studio but Paula Strasberg, her dramatic coach. Of course, she also had her new husband, the playwright Arthur Miller (their marriage – her third, his second – had taken place two weeks before they flew to England), but he had sworn not to interfere with the filming in any way.

Milton was Marilyn's partner and co-producer, but she didn't seem to be listening to him as much as she used to – probably because Miller resented the fact that Milton had once been her lover – so he needed all the allies he could get. I was only the third assistant director on the film – the person anyone can tell what to do – and as such I was hardly a threat to anybody, but Marilyn had always seemed quite sympathetic when I got yelled at, if indeed she noticed me at all. At the same time, I was Olivier's personal assistant, and I sometimes had access to him when Milton did not. So Milton had decided that he and I would be friends. On this occasion, he had probably guessed that what I really wanted was an excuse to go over to Marilyn's house; and he would have been right. After all, he spent half his time trying to stop anyone getting near Marilyn, because he knew that she was like a magnet that nobody could resist – not even a little assistant director, seven years younger than her. I should have been used to 'stars' by now. After all, Vivien Leigh and Margot Fonteyn were both family friends. But those two ladies, wonderful as they are, are both human beings. Marilyn is a true goddess, and should only be treated as such.

'I'm between a rock and a hard place, Colin,' said Milton. It was a glorious summer morning, but we had been awaiting Marilyn's arrival for over an hour, and he was getting impatient. 'Why can't Olivier accept Marilyn for what she is? You British think everyone should punch a timeclock, even stars. Olivier's disappointed because Marilyn doesn't behave like a bit-part player. Why can't he adapt? Oh, he's very polite on the surface, but Marilyn can see through that. She can sense that underneath he's ready to explode. Josh Logan* used to yell at her occasionally, but he worked with her as she was, and not as he wanted her to be. She's

---

* The director of *Bus Stop*, Marilyn's previous film.

---

scared of Olivier. She has this feeling that she'll never measure up.'

'Vivien says that Olivier fell for Marilyn's charm just like everyone else when he first met her,' I said. 'She says he even thought he could have a romance with her. And Vivien is always right.'

'Oh, Marilyn can charm any man if she wants to, but when she gets mad, it's a very different story. You watch out. By the way, what the hell has happened to her this morning?'

'I thought you said she shouldn't have to punch a timeclock.'

'Yes, but when it's her own money going down the drain – and mine . . .'

'I wouldn't mind if she kept us waiting all day. Working in a film studio is hot, boring, tiring and claustrophobic. I sympathise with Marilyn a lot.'

'Yeah, but it's her job.'

At that moment Marilyn's big black car came nosing round the studio block. It was instantly surrounded by a crowd of people who seemed to appear out of thin air. The new make-up man, the wardrobe mistress, the hair stylist, the associate director Tony Bushell, the production manager, all clamouring for attention before the poor lady could even get inside the building. She already had Paula Strasberg, with her script, and ex-Detective Chief Superintendent Roger Smith, late of Scotland Yard and protective as ever, carrying her bags. No wonder she fled inside like a hunted animal, taking no notice of Milton, or, of course, of me.

As soon as Marilyn had disappeared, with Milton trailing

behind her, I tackled Roger. I knew I had only a few seconds in which to explain. Roger returned to Parkside House as quickly as he could after dropping Marilyn off in the mornings, and David Orton, my boss on the studio floor, would soon be wondering where I was.

'I'm coming over to the house tonight to talk to Maria and José,' I said firmly. Maria and José were the Portuguese cook and butler I had hired to look after Marilyn at Parkside House. 'Milton says it's OK.'

'Oh yes? Problems, are there?' Roger looked sceptical.

'It won't take long, but we mustn't let them get upset. They would be terribly hard to replace. We can have a drink afterwards, and maybe a bite to eat. Ask Maria to make some sandwiches.'

Roger is devoted to Marilyn. After thirty long years in the police force, this is his finest hour. He follows her everywhere like a faithful Labrador dog. I'm not sure how much use he would be in a crisis, but he is clearly very shrewd, and with a bit of luck he could avert trouble before it occurred. I expect that he could see through my ploy, just as Milton had; but Roger has no one to talk to in the evenings, and he gets lonely. He reminds me of the drill sergeants I knew when I was a pilot-officer in the RAF, so we get on very well. All of the other people around Marilyn talk in film language, which Roger hates. He and I can have a gossip in plain English.

'So you don't need to come over to collect Marilyn this evening,' I went on. (There wouldn't be enough room in the car if he did.) 'I'll ride in the front with Evans, and then he can take me back.'

Evans is Marilyn's driver. Like Roger he had been hired by me, and he is one of the stupidest men I have ever met. I don't think he even knows who Marilyn Monroe is; but he does what he is told, which is the main thing.

'Hmm,' said Roger doubtfully, but just then a shout of 'Colin!' came from inside the building and I dashed away before he could reply.

I have known the Oliviers since I was a child, and I've met all sorts of famous people with my parents. But Marilyn is different. She is wrapped in a sort of blanket of fame which both protects and attracts. Her aura is incredibly strong – strong enough to be diluted by thousands of cinema screens all over the world, and still survive. In the flesh, this star quality is almost more than one can take. When I am with her my eyes don't want to leave her. I just can't seem to see enough of her, and perhaps this is because I cannot really see her at all. It is a feeling one could easily confuse with love. No wonder she has so many fans, and has to be so careful who she meets. I suppose this is why she spends most of her time shut up in her house, and why she finds it so hard to turn up at the studio at all, let alone on time. When she does arrive, she flashes from her car to her dressing room like a blur. She seems frightened, and perhaps she's right to be. I know I must not add to those persecuting her, yet I can't resist being in her orbit. And since I am paid by Olivier to make her life easier and smoother, I have to be in the background of her life, I tell myself, if nothing more.

As soon as I went inside the studio building I was in the usual trouble.

'Colin! Where the hell have you been?' David says this every time he sees me, even if I've only been gone for ten seconds. 'Olivier wants to see you straight away. It's 10 o'clock. Marilyn's only just arrived. We'll be lucky to get one shot done before lunch,' etc., etc.

Why don't they ever realise that, like it or not, this is Marilyn's pattern, and we might as well get used to it? Olivier argues that if we didn't make a fuss she'd never turn up at all, but I'm not so sure. Marilyn wants to act. She even wants to act with Olivier. She needs to make a success of this film to prove to the world that she is a serious actress. I think she'd turn up if the pressure was off. She might even be early, but I suppose that is a risk no film company would dare to take. Olivier talks about her as if she was no more than a pin-up, with no brains at all. He seems to have nothing but contempt for her. He is convinced she can't act – just because she can't clip on a character like a suit of clothes, in the way he can – and he despises her use of Paula as a dramatic coach. He can't see that Paula is only there for reassurance, not to tell Marilyn how to play the part. He only has to look at the film we've already shot to see that Marilyn is doing a very subtle job all on her own. The trouble is that he gets so frustrated by all the 'ums' and ahs', the missed cues and incorrect lines that he fails to recognise the flashes of brilliance when they come. Every evening the screenings of the previous day's filming remind him of the pain that he had to go through in front of and behind the camera, and he seems to take a perverse enjoyment in them. Why doesn't he get the editor to cut out all the horrors, and only show the bits that went well, however short? Imagine how exciting that would be. We all file into the viewing theatre; the lights go down; there is a thirty-second clip of Marilyn looking stunning and remembering all her lines; the lights go up again to a ripple of applause; Marilyn goes home encouraged instead of depressed; the editor is happy; Olivier is happy.

In your dreams, Colin! For some unknown psychological reason, blamed of course on technical necessity, we have to see every stumble and hesitation in giant close-up, repeated again and again, failure after failure, until we are all groaning and moaning, and Marilyn, if she has turned up, flees back to her house in shame. I just wish I could have a quiet chat with her and reassure her. But there are too many people already doing that – and patently failing.

I had only been over to Marilyn's house once since she moved in five weeks ago, and there was no point in thinking that I would get a chance to talk to her, or even to see her, if I went there again. All I wanted now was the excitement of riding in the front of the car, with this heavenly creature in the back. I wanted to feel as if I was her bodyguard, instead of Roger. I wanted to feel as if her safety depended on me. Luckily, Evans takes no notice of me whatsoever, and nor does Paula Strasberg. She has been 'coaching' Marilyn all day in the studio, but then there are sixty or so technicians there with her, not to speak of twenty other actors, and Olivier himself. In the car, Paula is only concentrating on getting Marilyn to herself for a few last minutes. She grips her arm fiercely and never stops talking, never draws breath, for the whole trip. She repeats herself again and again, pouring reassurance into Marilyn's ear: 'Marilyn, you were wonderful. You are a great, great actress. You are superb, you are divine . . .' and so on.

In the end, her praise of Marilyn's performance and acting ability gets so exaggerated that even Marilyn starts to get uneasy. It's as if Paula knows she only has this short moment in which to implant herself on Marilyn's mind for the night, and thus make herself indispensable for the following day.

Olivier, as the director of the film, naturally resents Paula's presence intensely. Paula knows nothing of the technical difficulties of making a movie, and often calls Marilyn over to give her instructions while Olivier is in the process of explaining to Marilyn what he needs, as the director. On these occasions Olivier's patience is really incredible. Nevertheless, I like Paula, and I feel sorry for her. This dumpy little woman, swathed in differing shades of brown, with her sunglasses on her head and her script in her hand, is clinging for dear life to a human tornado.

The only person who seems completely unaffected by all the hubbub is Arthur Miller, and perhaps that is why I dislike him so intensely. I must admit that he has never actually been rude to me. On the four occasions that our paths have crossed – at the airport when he and Marilyn first landed in England, on their arrival at the house I had rented for them, once at the studio and once out with the Oliviers – he has ignored me completely. And so he should. There is no one on the whole film crew more junior than I am. I am only present to make Marilyn's life, and therefore his life, run more smoothly.

And yet I don't quite think of myself as a servant. I'm an organiser, a fixer. Laurence Olivier takes me into his confidence. So does Milton Greene. But Arthur Miller takes it all for granted – his house, his servants, his driver, his wife's bodyguard, and even, so it seems to me, his wife. That is what makes me so angry. How can you take Marilyn Monroe for granted? She looks at him as if she worships him; but then, she is an actress. Vivien Leigh often gazes at Olivier like that, and it doesn't seem to do him much good. Miller just looks so damn smug. I am sure he is a great writer, but that doesn't mean that he should be so superior. Perhaps it's a combination of his horn-rimmed glasses, his high brow and his pipe. Added to all this there is a gleam in his eye which seems to say, 'I am sleeping with Marilyn Monroe, and you are not. You midget.'

All this was whirling round in my head as I jumped into the front seat of the car that evening. I had stocked up Olivier's dressing room with whisky and cigarettes, and told David that I had to go to Marilyn's house on an urgent mission, implying that I would be spying on her for Olivier. Since David is always trying to discover Marilyn's movements so that he can plan the filming schedule a little better, this seemed to him an excellent idea.

Speeding through the English countryside in the front of Marilyn Monroe's car I felt frightfully important; but as soon as we arrived at Parkside House Marilyn simply vanished inside, and that was that. Even Paula could not keep up with her. She must know that Arthur is going to take over from here on, and she followed slowly, looking very dejected, as if she had lost her child.

Roger came out of the house to meet me, grunting and chuckling, cheeks puffed out like a beardless Father Christmas, and together we went round towards the back entrance. Then, just as I had expected, Evans drove away. He had been sitting in the car since 6.30 that morning, and I'm sure that the last thing he wanted was to be given another job or errand.

'He was meant to wait and take me back to Pinewood!' I cried. 'Now I'm stuck here without a car. I'll have to walk to the village and catch a bus!'

'Don't worry,' said Roger patiently. 'As soon as they've settled down for the night' – jerking his head at the first-floor bedroom windows – 'I'll give you a lift. Come in and have your talk with José and Maria, and then we can have a drink and a smoke in my sitting room until the coast is clear.' This was a charade that we both understood. It would give us a chance to have a gossip, and to laugh at the crazy behaviour of everyone in the film world. I can sometimes do that with Olivier, but then I have to be careful how far I go. With Roger I can say absolutely anything and he will just smile and puff at his pipe – although he will never say a word against Marilyn herself, and any mention of Arthur just has him rolling his eyes.

Talking to José and Maria just meant listening to their problems for half an hour. They both speak very little English, and naturally nobody speaks Portuguese, although I can remember a little of what I learned when I was there the year before. I simply say '*Pois*' ('Yeah, sure . . .') whenever there is pause, and it usually works. On this occasion, however, the problems seemed more serious than usual, and I was forced to fall back on my schoolboy Latin to guess what on earth was going on.

'Meez Miller,' they said – they had been introduced to 'Mr and Mrs Miller' when Arthur and Marilyn arrived, and since they had never been to the cinema in their lives, they appeared to have no idea who they were – 'Meez Miller is sleeping on the floor.' They seemed to be saying, 'Is it because we make the bed wrong? We think it is our fault. If so, we should leave.'

This seemed to me pretty egotistical reasoning even by the standards of domestic servants. I told them that I would investigate, but that I was quite sure that they were not to blame.

'This house is "*louca*",' they said. 'Mad.' There was shouting in the middle of the night and silence in the middle of the day. Mr and Mrs Miller would not speak to them. Mrs Miller acted like she was in a dream.

I realised that it was time to be firm. 'That is no concern of yours,' I said sternly. 'Mrs Miller has a difficult job. She needs to conserve her energy very carefully. And she doesn't speak Portuguese, so she couldn't speak to you even if she wanted to. You must take no notice of her and Mr Miller. The company pays you good wages to look after Mr and Mrs Miller. We think you are the best – otherwise we could no longer ask you to stay.'

This policy worked. They both nodded nervously, and left the room as quickly as they could. I went in search of Roger.

'What's this, Roger old bean?' I asked when I had found him. 'Maria tells me that Marilyn is sleeping on the floor these days.'

Roger put a gnarled forefinger beside his nose and gave his usual chuckle. I'm never sure what this means. Sometimes he will follow it by saying, 'A nod's as good as a wink to a blind man,' which is equally confusing, if not more so.

'Trouble between Mr and Mrs M. already?' I asked. 'They've only been married a few weeks.'

'I've not heard either of them complain.' Roger gave a watery leer. 'But I have heard them playing trains at all hours of the night. No doubt about that.'

'Playing trains' was Roger's euphemism for making love in all its different forms.

'Doesn't sound a very amusing way of playing trains to me – sleeping on the floor.'

'Who said anything about sleeping?' said Roger

'Well, Maria . . .' I said.

'Maria can get it wrong. Just because there are bedclothes out there . . . What does Maria know? Marilyn's on her honeymoon. She can do what she likes. It isn't any business of ours. And now I'm going out to check the gardens for reporters in the bushes. You stay here until I get back, and then we'll go upstairs for a drink. But don't go exploring.' He had correctly read my mind. 'Arthur and Marilyn could still be downstairs, and Paula and Hedda' – Hedda Rosten, a New Yorker and former secretary of Arthur Miller, who was acting as Marilyn's 'companion' – 'are hanging around waiting for their supper, greedy things. Who would want them with them on their honeymoon, I don't know. Poor Marilyn. She's never allowed a moment's peace. No wonder she spends so much time in the bedroom.'

Another sly grin and he was gone.

'Yes, but it's her third honeymoon,' I said to his retreating back. 'She should know what to expect by now.'

When Roger got back from his rounds, it was clear that he didn't want to discuss the Millers any longer. He feels that it is disrespectful to do so, disloyal even. I'm sure that when he was in the police force loyalty to his colleagues was the most important thing in his life. Now all that loyalty goes to Marilyn. He has fallen under her spell, just like everyone else; but as a father, not a lover. One mustn't forget that somewhere there is a Mrs Roger, clucking over her knitting. I do hope she is as cosy as Roger is. When I hired him he told me that he had been married for over thirty years, and that he had a son my age. 'He's in the force now,' he said with pride.

We went upstairs to Roger's room, and he produced a bottle of Scotch and a couple of glasses. 'Here's to Marilyn Monroe Productions,' he said. Marilyn Monroe Productions paid him, but not me.

'Laurence Olivier Productions, more likely,' I replied, sitting down and lighting a cigarette.

'Roger,' I said, 'you know my job is to find out anything that might influence the progress of the film and pass it on to Olivier. So tell me, what's up?'

'Get stuffed, Colin,' said Roger amiably. 'My only job is to protect Marilyn, as you yourself told me when you hired me, and that is what I do. Why, only yesterday I caught one of those bloody reporters up a drainpipe outside Marilyn's bathroom. He'd managed to get over the fence and across the lawn, and he'd climbed the first set of pipes he saw. Another few minutes and he'd have been in Marilyn's toilet, and then she would have a got a surprise!' He gave another chuckle, then started on his favourite topic: the press. What he couldn't stand was that they were so cheeky. He had spent his life catching criminals – people who broke the law. Now he is confronted by a lot of men who have no respect for decent behaviour and are prepared to go to any lengths to get what they want, but who behave more like mischievous schoolboys than members of a criminal class.

'What can I do, Colin? I can't arrest them. I'm not allowed to thump them. All I can do is throw them out and wait for them to try again.' What Roger really wants is someone to make an assassination attempt on his beloved Marilyn, then he can save her in a heroic fashion. In the meantime the photographer from the *News of the World* is the enemy, and Roger has to deal with him.

When we had finished our whiskies, Roger went downstairs and reappeared with a plate of Maria's sandwiches and some bottles of beer. By 10.30 we were thoroughly relaxed, but it was getting dark outside and I still had to solve the problem of where I was going to spend the night. Roger was happy to drive me home, but I was not quite sure if he was up to it. His eyes had got very watery indeed, and his nose was alarmingly red.

'There's a spare room at the end of the corridor,' I said hopefully.

'I don't expect the bed is made up,' said Roger. 'Maria would have a fit if she found out you'd slept in it. And what would Marilyn think when you climbed into the car with me tomorrow morning?'

'I'm afraid she wouldn't even notice me. But you're right,

I'd better call a taxi.' I opened the door of Roger's room and peered out. The whole house was as silent as a tomb.

'Paula and Hedda go to bed at ten,' said Roger, 'and José and Maria will be in the servants' quarters by now, so you're perfectly safe. Do you know your way down?'

'Of course I do,' I said pompously. 'I've been to this house many times before. Don't forget that the owners are great friends of my parents.' (In fact I had been there only twice before, and upstairs only once.) 'I can use the phone in the kitchen. I saw the telephone number of the local taxi company on the wall. You go to bed, I'll be fine.' I slipped out of the door and shut it firmly behind me.

It is at these rather tense moments that Mother Nature so often pays a call. The question 'Should I turn left or right?' was soon supplanted by the absolute knowledge that I had about thirty seconds in which to find a lavatory. Actually, toilets in strange houses are not that hard to locate. At the tops of stairs, in little *cul de sacs*, they often give away their presence by a gentle but insistent hiss. It did not take me long, in my desperate condition, to locate an open door with a light switch conveniently placed on the wall just inside. But when I emerged, greatly relieved, a few moments later, a new problem presented itself. The lavatory light had been extremely – absurdly, I thought – bright. The rest of the house was now in absolute pitch darkness, and I was lost. I could just make out a thin line of light under one of the doors. That might indicate that it was Roger's room, but then again it might not. If I walked in on Paula or Hedda they would certainly think the worst. They might even welcome me, and then I'd really be in trouble. My heart beating wildly, I felt my way slowly along the corridor, sliding my feet along the carpet in case I reached a step. Eventually I got to a corner, and I stopped and peered round. Still I could see nothing. 'I must wait for my eyes to get accustomed to the dark,' I decided. 'I'll stand here for a full minute with my eyes tightly shut.'

It should have been a peaceful enough solution, but after a few seconds I became aware of a very strange thing. I was not alone. I could hear breathing, and it did not seem to be mine. It sounded more like a succession of little sighs. What was going on? Had I walked into somebody's bedroom? I held my breath, but the sighing went on.

Suddenly, a door at the far end of the corridor was flung open and a shaft of brilliant light flooded the scene. There, only a few feet in front of me, was Marilyn, sitting on the carpet with her back against the wall. If I had gone on for another few feet I would have fallen right over her. Now she simply sat there, wrapped in a pink bedcover, her head turned towards me, staring straight into my eyes. She did not give the slightest sign that she could see me. Were the shadows around me too deep? Had she been sleepwalking? Or was she drugged? There were many rumours floating around the studio of the number of sleeping pills she took.

She looked strangely fragile for the first time, and my heart went out to her with a rush. This ravishingly beautiful and vulnerable woman was literally at my feet. What could I do? I held my breath. I did not move a muscle.

'Marilyn.' Arthur Miller's voice seemed to come from another world. It made me jump backwards as though I had been shot. I must have made a noise, but at least I was now safely round the corner and out of sight.

'Marilyn. Come back to bed.' His tone was insistent but strangely flat, as if it were the middle of the day.

There was a pause. Marilyn didn't answer. Her breathing never varied. Long, slow intakes and then little sighs.

Arthur's voice came nearer. 'Come on. Get up. Time to go to sleep.' There was a rustle as Marilyn's bedcover fell to the floor. I couldn't hear their footsteps on the thick carpet, but soon a door shut and the bolt of light went out.

Only then did I realise that I was shivering. I felt I was in shock. My shirt was wet through with perspiration, as if I had been under a shower.

It seemed to take me an eternity to find the stairs, and by the time I got to the kitchen I was ready to faint. My emotions were in turmoil. I had never experienced anything like this before in my life. I couldn't get Marilyn's gaze out of my head. Marilyn Monroe, staring straight at me with that amazing sort of mute appeal. I could only dream of somehow saving her – but with what, and from what, I had no idea. I stumbled into the dining room and found a bottle of brandy on the sideboard. It was full, and I took a long swig, perhaps longer than was wise. That immediately brought on a fit of coughing which threatened to wake the whole house. The only answer seemed to be another swig. Then, for the third time that night, an unwelcome light snapped on.

'We'd better get you home straight away, laddie,' said Roger grimly, his dressing-gowned figure making for the phone. 'You're not going to be in much shape for work tomorrow. Never mind,' he added. 'I don't expect Marilyn will be going in anyway. I think I heard her still awake a minute ago. Let's just hope Mr Miller doesn't ask me who was coughing in the middle of the night.' He spoke into the phone: 'Hello, taxi? Can you come and collect someone from Parkside House, Englefield Green? Five minutes? Very well. We'll be outside. Don't whatever you do ring the bell.' He turned back to me. 'Come on, laddie. You're only twenty-three. You'll be OK. You'll be in bed in a flash. Don't fall asleep in the car, mind.'

And so on and so on, until he had wedged me unsteadily in the back of the car, taken a pound out of my wallet for the driver, and told him where to go.

When I finally got to bed I was exhausted, but I could not sleep. That image of Marilyn simply would not leave my mind. She seemed to be addressing me directly, like a figure in a dream, as if her spirit was calling out to mine.

Wed-nesday, 12 September

I expected to have a terrible hangover the next morning, but when the alarm went off I was still feeling strangely excited. It took a few minutes before reality set in. It was six o'clock in the morning and I was meant to be at Pinewood Studios, ten miles away, at 6.45.

If my car had been outside all would have been well. At this hour of the morning it only took fifteen minutes to get there. But I did not have my car, and although Marilyn never turned up at the studio on time, Olivier always arrived at seven o'clock sharp. Tony and Anne Bushell, with whom I was staying at Runnymede House, which they had rented for the duration of the filming, would not be getting up for another hour. They were kind and generous people, but they would not like to be woken at 6.30 a.m. and asked for a lift. Tony is the associate producer on the film, and he does not arrive on the set until nine. Only the actors need to get there so early, in order that they can be made up and put into their costumes before shooting starts.

I dressed quickly and went out into the morning air to seek inspiration. The events of last night now seemed like a crazy dream. It was almost as if they hadn't happened at all. I certainly could not give them as an excuse for being late for work. But then, to my delight, I noticed that there were two cars in the drive outside the house – Tony's Jaguar, and an elderly MG. That must belong to Anne's son Ned, I thought. He sometimes came down for the night. Desperate times call for desperate measures. I went back inside the house and went up to the spare room. Sure enough, there was Ned, very sound asleep.

'Ned,' I whispered in his ear. 'I need to borrow your car for a few hours. Is that OK?'

Ned snored on. He is my own age, and he must have had a weary night.

I picked up his trousers from the floor and took his car keys out of the pocket. There was no time to explain. I found a piece of paper on the desk and wrote: 'Sorry about the car – back soon. Colin,' and left.

'We don't have this car registered to you, sir,' the guard said when I arrived at the main gate of the studios. 'No car that isn't registered is allowed in. We can't be too careful now Miss Monroe is here. These reporters try all sorts of tricks.'

'I'm not a reporter, you fool. I'm assistant director on the film.'

'Sorry, sir. Just doing my job.'

Cursing, I had to leave the car on the grass verge and run down the long drive to the studio. The MG had not been as fast as my Lancia, and I was late.

'What happened to you, boy?' asked Olivier as I panted into his dressing room.

'My car broke down. I'll have to sort it out at lunchtime.' I didn't dare mention what had really happened. 'I don't think Marilyn will be in early,' I said. 'Roger told me she had a pretty disturbed night.'

'We'll have a pretty disturbed *day* if she doesn't show up. We shot all the simple stuff yesterday because she was so woolly. When is she going to recover her composure and start to work?'

'She's on her honeymoon, I suppose. Maybe that's affecting her.'

'Oh, nonsense, she's not a schoolgirl. And Arthur's getting fed up too. He told me he needs a holiday already.' Olivier grimaced. 'The trouble is that she's so damn moody, and she stays up most of the night. I pity Arthur. I wouldn't sleep with Marilyn for a million dollars, I can assure you of that.'

Nor her with you, I thought, but I said nothing.

Just before lunch, to everyone's surprise, and my great relief, Marilyn did show up after all. The usual bunch of people materialised out of thin air to pester the poor lady, but I only had eyes for Evans, the chauffeur. I did not have time to worry about whether Marilyn had seen me the night before or not, but I did most urgently need to get the MG back to Ned. Even so, I was anxious to avoid Marilyn's direct gaze. She wears very dark glasses when she first arrives at the studio, and one can never be quite sure how much she can see. By the time she was ready to start work, I imagined, she would be thinking of nothing but her lines.

'Where have you been?' asked David Orton suspiciously

as I slipped back onto the stage an hour later, Evans having driven me back from Runnymede House.

'Tummy upset,' I said.

He glowered, but I was home.

Filming that afternoon followed the now-familiar pattern. We all wait around the set under the 'work' lights for Marilyn to appear. Every quarter of an hour, Olivier tells David to go to Marilyn's dressing room to ask when she will be ready. David is a professional of the old school. He believes in a chain of command.

'Colin!' he shouts

'Yes, David?'

'Go to Miss Monroe's dressing room and ask when she will be ready.'

This of course is her portable dressing room, right there on the studio floor. From the outside, the thing looks like a caravan on a building site. Inside it is all soft lights and beige fabrics, like Parkside House.

I tap on the thin metal door. The make-up man or the wardrobe lady answers my knock. 'Not yet,' they whisper. It is as if we are all waiting for someone to give birth – and in a way, I suppose we are.

Finally, and without any warning, the doors fly open and Marilyn appears, looking absolutely gorgeous in the incredible white costume designed for her to wear in her role as the chorus girl Elsie Marina by 'Bumble' Dawson. Her head is held high, she has a little smile on her lips, her huge eyes are open wide, and her gaze is fixed upon the set. Marilyn is ready. Marilyn is going to do it now, or die in the attempt.

A shout from David. (David has, and needs, a very loud voice, as there are over fifty impatient people present.)

'Ready, studio!'

The film lights come on, one after another, with a series of terrific 'clunks'.

Marilyn looks startled. Paula, ever present an inch from her elbow, whispers something in her ear. Marilyn hesitates for a split second . . . and is lost.

Instead of going straight to her marks in front of the camera, she deflects to her 'recliner' positioned nearby. Paula, the make-up man, the hair stylist and the wardrobe lady all follow and re-surround her. Now she has to steel herself all over again, only this time the studio lights are burning away and we are poised to start work. If Marilyn loses her nerve completely, a scarlet flush, which she cannot control, spreads over her neck and cheeks, and then she has to go back to her dressing room and lie down. That means that the dress has to come off, and the wig has to come off, and it will be two hours before we can start the whole process again. It really is a miracle that anything ever gets done.

That afternoon it was clear that Marilyn was even more distressed than usual. By four o'clock she had left the set for the second time, and Olivier decided to call it a day. When I went into his dressing room to sort out the scripts – and the whisky and cigarettes – he was in an urgent discussion with Milton Greene as to what the cause of Marilyn's distraction could be.

'Don't you know anything, Colin?' Olivier asked me. 'You

hired her bodyguard. Can't you find out from him what's going on?'

'I know she and Arthur had an argument last night.'

'We all know that,' said Milton. 'She rang me at one a.m. to ask for more pills. I know I promised Arthur that I wouldn't involve him with filming problems, but I'm going to telephone him now and see if he'll tell me what's up.'

'You'd better wait outside, Colin,' said Olivier. 'But don't go away.'

When they called me in again five minutes later, both men were looking pale.

'It seems that Arthur Miller has decided to go to Paris tomorrow,' said Olivier stiffly. 'Evidently he has to see a literary agent there. Milton says this is the very worst thing for Marilyn. She has a horror of being deserted, even for a day. Both her previous husbands did it, and it terrifies her. She's driving me absolutely crazy, but I suppose she's giving Arthur a hard time too, so I can't say I blame him.'

'Marilyn is still in the studio,' I said. 'Perhaps she's too upset to go home.'

'Oh, God,' said Milton. 'Still in the studio at this time? I'd better go and see what she needs.'

He dashed out of the room, but he was back in under thirty seconds, looking very grim.

'Paula won't let me in. She says Marilyn won't see anyone, and she shut the door in my face.'

'Colin,' said Olivier, his voice like a spade in gravel, 'go across to Mrs Strasberg and ask her very politely whether Miss Monroe intends to come to the studio and work tomorrow. Don't go as my assistant. Say David needs to know.'

This was pretty high-risk stuff. A direct question. Usually Marilyn and Paula are already in the car back to Parkside before the rest of us have left the set. And of course they never answer the phone once they are home. Now, for the first time, they were still in our domain, at our mercy, as it were.

I marched across the thirty feet or so separating the suites of the two great stars and knocked on the door.

No reply. Cowardice means dismissal. Knock again!

The door opened a crack and Paula's eye appeared. She gazed at me for a full five seconds, in disbelief. Even from the little I could see of her, I could tell that she was in the grip of strong emotions.

'Come in,' she croaked, standing aside. I edged past her, and she closed the door firmly behind me.

She was alone in the pretty little sitting room that acted as a foyer to the *sanctum sanctorum* where Marilyn actually got dressed.

'Go in.' She closed her eyes and pointed to the door. 'Go in.'

'Go in?' I didn't understand what she meant. 'Go in where?' I felt like Alice through the looking glass. I'd never even been allowed in this reception room before, at least not when Marilyn was in it. This was holy ground. This was too much.

'Go in.' Paula pointed to the door again. 'Go in!'

The inner room seemed to be in pitch darkness. I took two steps inside and stopped.

'Colin.' Marilyn's voice was no more than a whisper, but every word was completely clear.

'Yes?'

'Shut the door.'

I closed the door behind me, and held my breath.

There was a long pause. I could see nothing. I felt as if I had dropped off the edge of the world and was falling through space. All I could hear was a succession of little sighs. The same sighs that I had heard last night.

'Colin?'

'Yes?' I found myself whispering too, I wasn't sure why.

'What were you doing in my house last night? Did they send you to spy on me?'

'Oh, no, Marilyn . . .' What was I thinking of? This was the greatest film star in the world. 'Oh, no, Miss Monroe. I came over to talk to the servants. I hired them for you, you see, when I found the house for you, you see, and they are always complaining about something, and I thought that if I went over and listened, they would calm down. And then I stayed and had a sandwich with Roger, you see, and when I came out of his room I got lost. I'm so sorry,' I ended in a rush.

Pause. As my eyes grew accustomed to the lack of light, I could just make out the figure of Marilyn in a white bathrobe, lying on a sofa against the wall. She had taken off her blonde Elsie Marina wig and she looked very frail.

'Colin?'

'Yes, Miss Monroe?'

'What is your job on the picture?'

'I'm the third assistant director. What they call a "gofer".

I have to go for this and go for that, whenever I'm told. Anyone can boss me around. I really hardly have a job at all.'

'Don't you work for Sir Laurence as well? I always see you round him. He seems to talk to you more than most of the others. Do you calm him down too, like you do the servants?' Marilyn chuckled.

'Oh, heavens, no. It's just that he's a friend of my parents, so I've known him for ages – since I was a child. I suppose I'm the only one who isn't frightened of him, that's all.'

Another long pause, while I struggled for breath.

The room was so still that I thought Marilyn might have fallen asleep. What an incredible contrast to the whirlwind that normally surrounded her. I wondered how often she managed to find solitude like that.

'Colin?'

'Yes?'

'Are you a spy? A spy for Sir Laurence? Tell me the truth.'

'I'm not a spy, Marilyn,' I said, plucking up all my courage. 'But it's my job to report to Sir Laurence anything that will help him to get this movie made as quickly as possible. I'm sure you want that too. The sooner it's over, the sooner you can go home to America. I'm sure you and Mr Miller are both looking forward to that. And now Sir Laurence has sent me to ask you if you are going to come into the studios tomorrow, and that's why I'm here,' I finished lamely, in case she thought I had just barged in.

'Mr Miller is flying to Paris tomorrow to see his agent,'

Marilyn said coldly. 'He may even go back to New York for a few days. I think I'll stay home and see him go.'

'Oh, of course, Miss Monroe. I quite understand. And so will Sir Laurence, I'm sure. Of course, of course, of course.' What a relief to be told outright, for a change. And perhaps with Arthur Miller out of the way, she might concentrate more on making the film. And on me! I knew I was being a complete fool, but I did have her total attention right at that moment, and the excitement in me rose.

'How old are you, Colin?'

'Twenty-five.' It was only a small lie, but I felt bad immediately. 'Nearly.'

There was another long pause. I seemed to have been in that room for hours. I began to wonder if Olivier and Milton Greene would still be at the studio when I got out. I hoped they wouldn't think that I had forgotten about them and gone home. They would certainly be very impatient. Everything to do with Marilyn seemed to take an incredibly long time, even though she was always in a rush.

'Colin.' Marilyn spoke so quietly that I had to step forward to hear her.

'Colin, whose side are you on?'

'Oh, yours, Miss Monroe. I promise you I'm on your side and I always will be.'

Marilyn sighed. 'Will you be coming to work tomorrow?'

'Well, yes. I come to work every day.' I didn't understand the question, but I was saved by a sharp tap on the door.

'Marilyn,' said Paula in honeyed tones, 'it's really time we went home.'

She opened the door wide, catching me standing on one leg in the middle of the room.

'Colin has to finish his work now,' she said. 'Don't you, Colin? Thanks for stopping by.'

She was like a mother hen fussing over her chick. She could hardly regard me as a wolf, but then again I wasn't exactly a baby chicken either. Marilyn gave another sigh. My interview was over.

As soon as I was out in the cold stone corridor of the studio, I found myself gasping for air. My first instinct was to rush along to Olivier's dressing room and report the whole thing. I felt incredibly pleased with myself. I'd asked Marilyn exactly what Olivier wanted to know, and I'd got an answer. Even better, I felt that I had established a rapport with Marilyn which might come in useful later on.

But wait one minute! Things weren't quite that simple now. Whose side was I on? Olivier was my boss. He was also, in some respects, an old friend. Uncle Larry. 'Boy', he called me most of the time. And Vivien was my heroine of all time. She was by far the most beautiful woman I had ever seen.

But Marilyn was different again. She was prettier than Vivien, younger, of course, and more vulnerable.

And she had appealed to me directly.

'Colin, whose side are you on?'

'Yours,' I had said. I could never go back on that. I marched down the corridor and knocked on Olivier's door.

'Come in.'

'Miss Monroe says she will not be coming to the studio tomorrow. Mr Miller is going to Paris and she wishes to spend the morning with him.'

'Did she tell you this herself?' Milton was incredulous.

'Yes.'

'Is that all she said?'

'Yes.'

Both men looked at me with curiosity. For the first time ever, they were actually taking notice of what I said. I have Marilyn to thank for that, I thought, as I turned and went out. I know whose side I'm on now.

Thursday, 13 September

All film crews take a pride in being cynical. The more well-known the stars they work with, the more the crew affects an air of studied indifference whenever the famous person appears. The team working on *The Prince and the Showgirl* is even more professional than most. They have been hand-picked by Olivier and his production manager Teddy Joseph so that they will not ogle Miss Monroe, or try to catch her eye. At the same time, they have strong views about the actors and actresses they work with, and there is a rigid pecking order which all crews observe.

Minor actors, and even major ones in supporting roles, are totally ignored.

British stars in British films, like Anthony Steel or Maureen Swanson, who are both working on other films at Pinewood at the moment, are treated as complete equals – just as if they were also technicians, merely doing a different job.

Great British stage actors, like Dame Sybil Thorndike, who is playing the Queen Dowager, the mother of Olivier's character the Regent of Carpathia, are given exaggerated courtesy, as if they were honoured visitors to the set and not participants. The Oliviers, Laurence and Vivien, are a special case, treated like royalty and spoken of in hushed tones. Olivier is always referred to as 'Sir', although not to his face. Lady Olivier is called 'Vivien', even to her face – but, oh, with what respect and awe.

Big Hollywood stars are treated with complete nonchalance, but each one is given an approval rating in the endless gossip which takes place while the crew is waiting for them to appear. Marilyn is different altogether. She is now so famous, and it is so tempting to look at her, that everyone avoids her gaze as if she had the evil eye. I am not sure if she is too happy about this. She obviously does not have much self-confidence, and I think she prefers a group of men to applaud and smile when she walks into a room, rather than to look away.

Whatever they may pretend they are doing, however, every man and woman in Studio A is keeping one eye on Marilyn every moment she is there. They can't resist, and endless Marilyn stories, Marilyn rumours and Marilyn jokes make the rounds. On the mornings when she does not show up, the crew get slack and sit around with glum faces, like children who have not been invited to a party.

This morning, for lack of anything else to amuse them, they've decided it's time to tease Colin.

'Colin is Marilyn's new boyfriend, I hear.'

'Just barges into her dressing room for a chat any time he likes, they say.'

'And how does Larry feel about that, I wonder.'

'He's jealous.'

'Of him, or of her?'

Gales of laughter.

'Look,' I said, '"Sir" simply told me to ask Miss Monroe whether she was coming to the studio today, so I knocked on her dressing-room door and asked her, and she said "No." That was all there was to it.'

'Oh? Norman [one of the hair stylists] said you were in there for ten minutes. Plenty of time for a cuddle.'

'Oh, yes. A cuddle with Paula, I suppose you mean. She was in there too. I presume Norman will confirm that.'

Jack Cardiff, the lighting cameraman, who has worked on such films as *The Red Shoes* and *The African Queen*, walked over to see what the fuss was about. Jack is the only person on the set who treats Marilyn like a chum. As a result he is the one crew member to whom she can relate, and certainly the only Englishman she trusts. In return he uses all his artistry to bring out her beauty. He clearly adores her, and because he is an artist, with no ulterior motive, she responds to him very well. The whole crew understand this and appreciate it. Jack, they can see, is the man who will save the film by putting Marilyn's radiance on the screen.

'Isn't Marilyn allowed to make friends?' said Jack. 'I wish the rest of you would be a bit more welcoming. She's a stranger here, you know, and no one is stranger than you lot. Let's get back to work.'

The truth is that the crew look at me with a good deal of suspicion. This is my first film, and I am very wet behind the ears. It was obviously Olivier himself who got me the job, and he treats me as if I was his nephew (although he often yells at me if I make a mistake). Vivien, who I have known since I was a boy, always singles me out when she visits. 'Colin, darling, are you looking after Larrykins for me?' she purrs, knowing full well that she embarrasses me as much as she pleases me. Dame Sybil also knows my parents. She treats me as if I was her grandson, and bought me a lovely thick wool scarf to keep me warm while I wait outside the studio at dawn to welcome the stars. (Come to think of it, Dame Sybil treats the whole crew as if they were her grandchildren, and would buy each one of them a woolly scarf if she could.)

Marilyn does not know my parents (thank God!), and there is no reason for her to talk to me at all. We have had a few cosy moments together (cosy for me, that is) when I have given her cues from behind the set, but otherwise she has always seemed to look straight through me as if I were a pane of glass. And so she should. The poor woman has enough on her plate without me making demands on her. I have to keep reminding myself that she is the most famous film star in the world, trying to keep up with the most famous actor in the world – and he is not the easiest man to please.

With Marilyn off the set we spent a boring day preparing to do the exterior shots, and it was not until 5.30 in the evening that I got to Olivier's dressing room to check with him before he left for home. Milton was already there, and they had obviously, from the state of the whisky bottle and the ashtray, had another of those long and intense conferences that seemed to lead nowhere at all.

'We've decided to give Marilyn another day off

tomorrow,' said Olivier firmly. 'Milton says she's upset about Arthur's departure, and now she can have a long weekend to pull herself together. One rather wonders,' he continued grimly, 'if she ever asks herself why so many people need a break from her presence.'

'That's not fair, Larry. Perhaps she needs a break from us,' said Milton. He is never malicious about anyone, except possibly Paula, and he'd certainly never dare even to think unkind thoughts about Marilyn.

'Quite so, dear boy,' said Olivier. 'Well, let us say that she can rest, and take a little time to learn her lines.'

I was wondering what on earth Marilyn would do in that big house, all alone with Paula for a long weekend, when the phone rang. Milton happened to be standing next to it, and he picked it up. He practically lives on the telephone, so whenever it rings he always assumes it will be for him. And it usually is, often from the USA.

'Milton Greene. Oh, Roger. Everything OK? Whaddya want?'

Suddenly his face seemed to crumple a little. 'Yes. He's here.' He looked at me.

'It's for you.'

'For me?'

Olivier nearly exploded. 'Who is Roger? What the hell's going on?'

I took the phone. 'What's the matter, Roger?'

'Colin.' Roger sounded very formal. 'Miss Monroe wants you to come via Parkside House on your way home this evening.'

'Me? Why me? Is Marilyn OK?' I asked.

Giggle. 'I'm OK,' said Marilyn's voice cheerfully. 'In fact I'm standing right here!'

If Milton had had false teeth he would have swallowed them. Like a trained dog, he had caught the unmistakable inflexion of his mistress's voice, and his mouth froze in terror.

'Who the fuck is on the bloody telephone?' roared Olivier, naturally furious at being excluded.

'It's Marilyn,' whispered Milton.

'MARILYN?'

'Monroe.'

'Yes, I know who Marilyn is, for God's sake.'

I heard Marilyn giggle again at the other end of the line.

'But what is my star doing phoning my third assistant director in my dressing room?'

'That's my boy,' said Marilyn. 'See you later, Colin. OK?'

'Very well, Miss Monroe. If you say so.'

Mercifully she hung up before I got fired.

'Miss Monroe was just ringing to tell me that she will not be coming to the studio tomorrow.'

'We knew that,' spluttered Olivier. 'And why is she telling you, and not me?'

'Well, you sent me into her dressing room to ask that question yesterday, so I assume she thinks you want me to be the messenger about that sort of thing.'

'Hmph! Well, what else did she say?'

'Nothing.'

'Colin, I heard her say something else.'

'She heard your voice in the background, asking who was on the phone.'

As always, Olivier forgot that he had just roared and swore.

'What did she say?' It was Milton's turn now, and he was pleading. Goodness knows why he is so scared of Marilyn. She had sounded very jolly to me.

'She asked me to pass on the message to Sir Laurence. That was all.'

'Oh, my God, Colin, you've got to be so careful with Marilyn,' said Milton. 'She gets upset very easily, if one is the least bit over-familiar.' He turned to Olivier. 'I don't know if Colin should talk to her any more, Larry. He's so young he could easily put his foot in it. She's not too keen on Brits right now anyway.'

Olivier's eyebrows shot up.

'Colin's very British, and he doesn't realise how important it is that Marilyn thinks we all love her.'

Milton was tripping over himself in his anxiety. He was like some feeble-minded courtier of Elizabeth I when the Spanish Armada was near. 'Off with his head,' if I was the Queen, I thought.

But Olivier got the point. 'Well done, Colin,' he said. 'Keep up the good work, and keep me informed. Now get us some more whisky, won't you, there's a good lad.' And I fled.

It was seven o'clock before I got to Parkside House. I had been seriously tempted to stop at a pub on the way, but in the end I decided that I had better not arrive smelling of whisky with an idiotic grin on my face. A good messenger needs a clear head. I parked my car round the corner of the drive and went in by the servants' entrance. Roger was sitting in the kitchen, looking rather serious.

'Miss Monroe says for you to wait in the drawing room,' he said gruffly, and took me through. 'Sit down, I would.'

Nothing happened for a very long time. I got up and prowled round the room, looking at it carefully for the first time. The french windows gave out onto a garden in full bloom, complementing the flowers on the wallpaper and the curtains.

Had Marilyn ever sat in it, I wondered. There was no evidence that she had. Roger said that she and Arthur spent most of their time upstairs, which I suppose meant in the bedroom. I had seen that when I inspected the house before renting it. It was part of a large suite which included a little sitting room so that they could eat up there whenever they wanted complete privacy – which was probably always, I thought. After all, they were on their honeymoon. Even though they were both quite old, this must still count for something. But I couldn't imagine what they talked about together. They seemed such different types. The attraction of opposites, I supposed. And now Arthur had gone off to Paris on his own. That didn't seem a very good sign.

The door to the hall opened, and Paula Strasberg put her head in.

'Oh, hi, Colin,' she said without much enthusiasm, and went away without asking what I was doing there, which seemed a little strange. A little later Hedda Rosten walked in from the garden. She is meant to be Marilyn's companion, but I have never seen them together. She is a middle-aged American lady with a nice face, but she drinks quite a lot, and she smokes, which Marilyn does not. Now she looked at me closely and opened her mouth as if to speak, but she evidently decided not to say anything, so I just smiled and she went out.

By now I was beginning to feel like a fish in a bowl. What on earth was I doing in Marilyn Monroe and Arthur Miller's house at eight o'clock on a Thursday evening? Marilyn had told me that she wasn't coming to the studio next day. She had tomorrow and all weekend to get a message to Olivier. Had she lost faith in Milton Greene to communicate with her director? Was I being put to some test? Why had those two ladies come in to have a look at me? Were they going to report back to Marilyn, I wondered, or were they just curious?

By this time I had been waiting for over an hour. It was just getting dark, and I was beginning to feel annoyed. I'll have that glass of whisky after all, I thought, and I went across to the tray with the bottles and the ice.

'Have a drink, Colin.'

Marilyn had come into the room without me hearing her.

'Oh, no. I'm sorry, Miss Monroe. I was just checking to see if you have everything you need.'

'I think so. I've only been in this room once, on the day we arrived from New York. It's very pretty in here, isn't it? Go ahead and have a drink if you want. Do you drink a lot, Colin? You don't look old enough to drink.'

'I'm really quite old, Miss Monroe,' I protested.

She was standing by the window in the half-light, wearing light silk trousers and a brown silk shirt which emphasised the fabulous Monroe bust. I had to admit that she looked absolutely stunning, but just for a minute the unworthy thought entered my head that perhaps she had delayed her entrance on purpose until the light had grown dim.

'Are you frightened of me, Colin?'

Terrified, I thought.

'No, I'm not.'

'Good, because I like you. You don't seem to want anything from me' – 'Umm,' I thought – 'and I want you to help me. Will you help me?'

'Well, I'll do anything I can, but I'm very unimportant. It's only because I'm Sir Laurence's personal assistant that I can talk to the cameraman and people like that. I'm really just a messenger, you see, more than anything else.'

'But you can see what's going on, can't you Colin? You can see both sides.'

Marilyn walked over to the sofa and sat down, stretching out her legs on the cushions beside her.

'Sit down and tell me everything that's going on.' She pointed to an armchair by her feet, and reluctantly I perched on the edge.

'Come on, Colin,' Marilyn laughed. 'I thought you said you weren't scared. Relax and let it out. Tell you what – let's have some dinner. I'm starved. Aren't you? I'll ask them to bring a tray of food.' Suddenly she seemed to get flustered. 'Or are you meant to be having dinner with someone else? Oh, gee, I'm sorry. Am I interrupting something?' Marilyn opened her eyes very wide and parted her lips, almost causing me to faint. 'There's not a Mrs Colin is there, waiting for you at home?'

'No, there's no Mrs Colin. And I am very hungry, but I'd like to make a phone call. I'm staying with the associate producer, Tony Bushell, and his wife, and they'll be expecting me for dinner.'

'Go right ahead and call,' said Marilyn. 'I'll go to the kitchen and see what they have.'

There was a telephone on the desk by the window. I dialled Tony's number.

'Bushell,' he barked. It had been many years since he was in the army, but he had acted as an officer in so many films about the war that he had permanently adopted a military manner.

'It's me,' I said. 'I can't come for dinner tonight.'

'Anne will be furious. The food is practically on the table. Where are you?'

'I'm at Parkside.' It was dangerous to tell him too much. Like David and almost everyone else at the studio, Tony was my boss. Marilyn Monroe had become 'the enemy' to him as soon as it was clear that she, unlike him, would not slavishly obey Olivier's every command. Nevertheless, being at Parkside was the one excuse that he could not ignore.

'At Parkside? What the hell are you doing at Parkside? Have the servants threatened to walk out? Are you going to cook Miss Monroe's dinner?'

'Not exactly . . .' I was stuck. I couldn't say that Marilyn was giving me messages for Olivier. Tony would have insisted that they should go via him. And he would certainly have rung Milton Greene and reported the situation immediately. I felt I was getting on really well with Marilyn, and I did not want Milton turning up to protect his investment – which he would have done at the speed of light.

'Miss Monroe has some large packages . . .' to my horror

I saw Marilyn come back into the room. I made an agonised face. '. . . which she wants to be sent to America . . .' Marilyn started to giggle. '. . . and I am waiting to collect them.'

'Can't Roger handle it?' Tony asked, just as Milton had two days earlier. 'Oh well, if you're stuck, you're stuck. She keeps everyone waiting. I'll explain to Anne,' and he hung up, grumbling.

'Now, Colin,' said Marilyn, sitting down on the sofa again. 'What is going on?'

Oh, all right then, what the hell!

'I'll tell you what is going on,' I said, going back to my armchair. 'We are all trying to make a film which absolutely should not be made. That is why it is such agony for everyone. Agony for you – we can all see that – and agony for Laurence Olivier too. You are a great film star who needs to prove that you can act. Olivier is a great actor who wants to be a film star. For some reason somebody has chosen a script where you play an American chorus girl, which is the sort of part you've played before and does not challenge you at all, and Olivier plays a stuffy old man, which is the opposite of what he wants to be. The whole thing is based on a play which I saw a few years ago in the theatre, with Olivier and Vivien Leigh, and it wasn't that good even then. It was a comedy of manners, and those never translate too well to the screen. I suppose somebody hoped it would be like one of those Spencer Tracy–Katharine Hepburn movies, but our script is stifled by all that old-fashioned dialogue, and all the costumes and the sets. It's such a pity, because you and Olivier both deserve roles you can get your teeth into.'

Marilyn was staring at me with surprise.

'They told me this was a great script – and I wanted to act with Olivier, so people would take me seriously. This was the only way to get him to agree to act with me.'

'Well, I think you were taken for a ride.'

'Gee, Colin, you really care, don't you? What are we going to do?'

This was, of course, the question which all of us had been asking ourselves ever since filming began, and I didn't have the answer any more than anyone else. Luckily I was saved from having to reply by the entrance of Maria and José, each carrying a large silver tray. They did not seem the least bit surprised to see me sitting there, which rather reassured me. They simply set down the food on the coffee table and waited.

'I'll have a Coke,' said Marilyn.

José looked at me.

'*Duas Colas. Frescas se fash favor.*'

'Ooh, do you speak the same language as them?' Marilyn was greatly impressed.

'It's Portuguese. I've been to Portugal a few times.'

'Ooh.'

There was a pause.

I looked at Marilyn across the table – and for the first time I realised what was going on. Marilyn was lonely. She needed someone to chat to, someone who would make no demands, someone who didn't expect her to be great or grand or clever or sexy, but just to be whatever she felt she wanted to be. Most of the time, I suddenly realised, she was incredibly tense. It was almost impossible for her to relax.

Now, because I was so much younger than her, she felt that I would not judge her, and she probably wouldn't care if I did.

Marilyn began to tuck into a large bowl of chicken mayonnaise, and it was obvious that she was extremely hungry. Those pills of hers probably suppress her appetite, I thought, as well as wake her up. Since she slept so late in the morning, this might well be her first meal of the day.

José returned with four bottles of Coca-Cola, two glasses and a bowl of ice.

'*Obrigado*,' I said.

'Ooh,' said Marilyn. She seemed to get more cheerful with each mouthful of food. 'Why couldn't you tell Mr Bushell you were here on a visit? What would he say?'

'He would explode, and kick me out of his house. He's a wonderful man, really, but he's totally blinded by his loyalty to Sir Laurence. If you are not 100 per cent loyal to Sir Laurence – as most of the film crew are, I must admit – you are the enemy as far as Mr Bushell is concerned.'

Marilyn chuckled. 'So I'm the enemy, am I? Well, don't worry, I won't give you away. After all, it's not as if we were having an affair.' More chuckles. 'But what are we going to do about the film?'

'There is nothing that can be done at this stage. It's too late to do anything but try to finish it, and make it as big a success as possible. Then go on to something better, I guess.'

'I thought I could do a great job,' said Marilyn, 'but every time I walk into that studio I get the creeps. Paula is the only person I feel I can trust. Except for you, maybe?'

She swivelled her body round on the sofa until her face was beneath mine, and looked up at me. Her eyes were so wide that I felt I was gazing down into a beautiful swimming pool, but before I could do anything about it there was a tap at the door, and someone walked in.

'Yeah?' said Marilyn, without moving a muscle.

'There is a telephone call for you, ma'am,' said Roger impassively. 'I think it is from abroad.'

Marilyn got up with a jolt.

'Gee,' she said. That vague blurred look was back in her eyes, and her shoulders had curved in. 'Well, goodnight, Colin. It was so nice of you to come over. I'd love it if you could come by tomorrow evening so we could continue our chat.' She shot out of the room like a frightened rabbit.

'You'll be leaving now, I expect,' said Roger, waiting by the door.

'Yes. Time to go,' I said, as nonchalantly as I could, and strolled out to my car without my feet touching the ground, as far as I could tell.

'Goodnight, Roger.'

'Humph.'

Tony and Anne were asleep by the time I got back to Runny-mede House, and I left before they woke up the next morning. It was not until 9.30 a.m. that the reverberations from the previous night began in earnest.

'Tony wants you to go to Sir Laurence's dressing room right away,' said David. 'And by the way he's roaring and stamping, you'd better brace yourself for a row. What were you up to last night, I wonder.'

'Nothing, I promise you. I can't think what it's about. I just missed dinner, that's all.'

'Ah, now. Missed dinner.' David squeezed up his face in an effort to look cunning. 'I wonder why?'

'I don't care if he is fucking her sideways,' I heard Olivier say as I walked into his room. 'Perhaps it will calm her down.'

(Olivier's language is always terrible. Jack Cardiff told me that when he first said 'fuck' in front of Marilyn, she opened her eyes very wide and said, 'Gee, do they have that word in England too?')

'Ah, Colin,' Olivier went on, without a pause. 'Tony tells

me you spent last night with Marilyn. Did you learn anything?'

'Spent last night with Marilyn!' I said indignantly. 'I spent last night in Tony's house. I just went over to Parkside to do an errand for her, and stayed for a chat. And what I learned is that she is not nearly as dumb as she looks.'

'And dinner,' interrupted Tony. 'You stayed for dinner too?'

'Marilyn was having chicken salad and she offered me some too, that's all.'

'What is more, I thought I heard her chuckle when you were on the phone. Marilyn doesn't usually chuckle. What was that all about?'

'Chuckling sounds good to me,' said Olivier.

'Yes, but Larry, this is a very sensitive situation,' said Tony. 'Colin is young and inexperienced. He might say something which would upset the whole apple cart. It took a year of secret planning to get Monroe over here, and one chance remark from Colin, even if he didn't know what he was doing, might send her and Arthur scurrying back to America.'

'Arthur's probably on his way back to America already,' I said. 'And I haven't made any chance remarks yet.'

'Perhaps,' said Olivier, 'if Colin is as nice and diplomatic as he can possibly be, Marilyn will be more likely to stay.' He gave me what looked almost like a leer.

'Miss Monroe simply treats me like a chum. Is there anything wrong with that?' I protested. 'She thinks I'm just a schoolboy.'

'Miss Monroe can be very manipulative if she wants to

be,' said Tony. 'She had Laurence eating out of the palm of her hand in New York, and now she treats him as if he didn't exist. You must be very careful indeed, Colin. She is a very dangerous lady. Very ambitious, and very ruthless too. You know she had another dramatic coach before Paula Strasberg, and when she got fed up with her she just dropped her like a hot potato – after pretending that she relied on her for many years. She is not afraid to use people in order to get what she wants. Don't believe anything she says. Those great big eyes are really weapons.'

Was Tony afraid that I'd upset Marilyn, or that Marilyn would hurt me?

'I don't exactly see how she could use me to further her career,' I said. 'I don't have any power over her one way or another. I just go over to Parkside to run errands. But I think last night she was lonely, with Arthur gone away, and she simply wanted to chat to someone who didn't boss her around. Paula is too sycophantic, and Hedda gets tipsy in the evenings. Anyway, I'll probably never get invited over again.'

'Well if you do, be very careful,' chorused the two men.

'And I presume you will be coming back to Runnymede House for dinner tonight,' added Tony, menacingly.

Somewhere in my mind I could hear Marilyn's voice saying, 'I'd love it if you could come by tomorrow evening,' as she had rushed to answer the phone, but she was probably only being polite.

'I'll be back for dinner tonight, I promise.'

Film sets are like pressure cookers – sealed, airless and incredibly hot. There are endless unexplained delays.

Rumours go round the crew in a matter of seconds. By the time I got back to my normal post by David's side, I had become the main object of attention again.

'Arthur hasn't been gone long then, Colin,' somebody called.

'What are you talking about?' I said, blushing furiously.

'Mrs Miller coming in today, is she? Or is she too tired?'

A chorus of cheers.

'Can't Marilyn show a little friendship without you clowns jumping to conclusions?'

'Oh, it's "Marilyn" now, is it?'

'That's the first time I've heard it called "showing a little friendship".' Etc. etc.

Richard Wattis, the actor who is playing Mr Northbrook of the Foreign Office, came over to give me some advice. Dicky is what you might call a confirmed bachelor, so I could guess what he was going to say.

'Have you heard of a flower called the Venus fly trap, Colin? Well, you are the fly. You think you can just buzz around, minding your own business, when suddenly a heady scent attracts you, and "Snap!" that's the end of you. Believe me, she is a very dangerous woman. I'm an actor. I know.'

'Oh, phooey to the lot of you,' I said. 'She is just a pretty girl who has got a bit out of her depth. Just imagine the pressure she is under, especially with you lot following her every move.'

'Give Marilyn a break,' said Jack Cardiff, coming to my rescue again. 'She's doing the best she can. You are all far too quick to gang up against her. She's the most beautiful woman I've ever photographed,' he said to me. 'And a very lovely person too.'

Finally, Olivier walked in, and everyone shut up and began to work.

As soon as we broke for lunch, however, it was Milton Greene's turn. For the first time he was waiting for me, rather than for Olivier, in the dressing-room corridor.

'Colin, I must talk to you very seriously.'

'Oh, goodness, not now, Milton. Sir Laurence is getting awfully irritated by all this. What on earth is the matter? I haven't done anything wrong.'

'I had a call from Arthur Miller in Paris last night. He was quite upset.'

'Arthur Miller! He doesn't even know who I am.'

'He does now. It seems he called Marilyn late last night, and she took a long time to come to the phone. When he asked her why, she said she had been saying goodbye to you.'

'Oh, she is naughty. I suppose she was cross with him for going away and decided to make him jealous. It wasn't late, it was about nine o'clock.'

'Ten-thirty, according to Arthur.'

How time had flown, to be sure.

'He's on French time. They're one hour ahead,' I said, thinking fast.

'That's not the point,' said Milton. 'Arthur wanted to know what you were doing there at all. And I couldn't tell him. What *were* you doing there? Tell me the truth.'

'I wasn't doing *anything*! Such a lot of fuss over absolutely nothing. Miss Monroe asked me to come over so she could give me a message for Sir Laurence. She kept me waiting for an hour or so, then she offered me some chicken salad, and then I left. That's all.'

'And what was Miss Monroe's important message for Sir Laurence which you had to deliver?'

'Well, it was just that she wasn't coming to the studio today.' It did sound a little lame.

'Something that Olivier already knew, right? In fact, it was Sir Laurence who told Marilyn that she needn't come in.'

'Well, er, yes. That's true, I suppose. I thought it was a little odd.'

'*Thought*? You didn't think at all, did you? If you'd "thought", you would have realised that you can't even go near someone as important as Marilyn Monroe without upsetting someone else. In this case, her husband. And me.'

Milton suddenly got friendly.

'Now, Colin, please don't go over to see Marilyn again. Or even talk to her without informing me first. She is completely, totally, off-limits to you and everyone else on the crew. Got that? I like you, Colin, but if this happens again I'll have to tell Sir Laurence that you must be banned from the studios completely. Sorry, but that's the way it is. I'm going over to have dinner with Marilyn myself this evening, and I'll explain the situation to her, so you don't need to call on her. She told Arthur that she might see you again tonight, and clearly that must not happen, tonight or any other night. OK?'

'OK, Milton. But I still think you're making a mountain out of a molehill.'

It had been fun while it lasted, but I did not want to lose my job. Nothing had happened, but I felt desperately sorry for Marilyn. The poor lady was completely trapped by her own fame. An innocent from California, trapped by all those crafty New Yorkers – a golden goose shut in a golden cage and forced to lay golden eggs for them all to enjoy. Arthur was the wicked king who kept her locked up in his castle. Milton was the magician who made sure she did what she was told. Paula was the corrupt courtier who poured endless soothing words into her ears, to fool her into think-ing that she was really the one with the power. The rest of us – including Olivier, although he didn't realise it – were just part of the scenery. All the trappings of being a great star were a total sham – literally, in the case of this film, nothing but a façade. Now the princess had tried to tell the world she was a prisoner. That was the real message Marilyn wanted to give me. And, naturally, that was exactly what all those greedy men did not want anyone to find out. No wonder Milton had tried so hard to warn me off.

I wanted desperately to save her, but what could I do? I couldn't tell the police. I couldn't tell a newspaper. No showbiz journalist would want to believe me – and anyway, they were all in on the plot. They were much too frightened of the establishment to rock the boat. Marilyn was like a prize cow, to be shipped from show to show, primped and polished and prodded while the audiences jeered and cheered. If she took one tiny step of independence, the sky would fall in. 'She is a dangerous, manipulative woman,' they would say, like Tony. 'You can't trust her an inch.'

Olivier was still in his dressing room when Milton left,

and in desperation I decided to try to discuss the problem with him. Olivier is a human being, I thought, a wonderful, loyal and sensible man. Perhaps if I explained the matter properly . . .

'Forget it, Colin,' he said before I could even speak. 'This thing is bigger than all of us. That's why I hate Hollywood so much. The studios there are so powerful that everyone is scared. It's just a great big money-making machine. They call it a dream factory. It is a factory; but not about dreams, just about money. Power, sex, glamour – those things just dazzle the public and conceal the truth. And girls like Marilyn are trying to exploit it, just as it is exploiting them. It's a war. No quarter given on either side. Believe me, you have to be pretty tough to get one tenth of the distance Marilyn has got. Now she has become the most famous star of them all. She took on the Hollywood bosses, and with Milton's help, she won quite a victory. For a while she even thought she was free. But who really controls her? MCA, the biggest Hollywood agency. Who pays for this film? Warner Brothers. Who does she still have a contract with? Twentieth Century-Fox. She just can't work without Hollywood's help and Hollywood's approval. Of course she'd like to have you as a chum, but it's too late for that. There are no chums in Hollywood. Just thank God that it isn't like that over here yet. Now go home to dinner with Tony and Anne. They are genuinely fond of you, you know.'

'Thanks, Larry,' I said, and went home with a heavy heart.

Saturday, 15 September

It was an absolutely glorious summer morning, and for once I did not have to get up at six a.m. to go to the studio. When I finally came downstairs, Anne Bushell was in the kitchen preparing lunch. She watched dubiously as I helped myself to cornflakes and milk.

'Tony tells me you've had quite an exciting week,' she said finally.

'It's been blown up out of all proportion,' I said. 'Do you really think it's such a dreadful sin to make friends with Marilyn? She doesn't have many friends, and Arthur's gone away and she's lonely.'

'That's where the danger lies, I suppose, Colin. You do have a bit of a reputation for chasing the ladies. Didn't I hear Tony talking about a girl in the wardrobe department? And some ballerina in London?'

'Oh, Anne, surely it's not a crime to admire beautiful women? I'm not having an affair with anybody, you know.' Anne was very attractive herself.

'Well, Marilyn is not just *any* beautiful woman, is she? There's a lot of money riding on her, you know. There's this film, and poor Larry's reputation as a director as well. And don't forget that she's on her honeymoon. That's definitely not the time for her to start making new young male friends. I heard that she had a terrible row with Arthur the other night. I hope it wasn't about you.'

'Of course not. Perhaps Marilyn doesn't like the way Arthur looks at her – as if she was a prize that he'd won in a raffle. She seems rather scared of him to me. She treats him like a very strict father whom she adores but can never quite please. Why he's gone to Paris I can't imagine. It may have been pre-arranged – they would be over in Europe anyway, and all that – but the rumour is that he's going back to New York before he returns here.'

'Oh, poor girl,' said Anne. 'She must be miserable.'

Just then I heard the noise of a car, and I went out to see who had come to visit. To my surprise there was Roger's elderly black Wolsey crawling up the gravel drive. Had he bought it when he retired from the police, I wondered. His faithful steed.

Tony had heard the arrival too, and strode out from behind the house to investigate.

'What's the problem, Roger?' he barked. Tony liked a problem. His military manner gave everyone the impression that he could cope in an emergency. In fact he was just an actor, and he always missed the point.

'No problem at all, Mr Bushell,' said Roger. 'I've just come over to take Colin out to lunch.'

'Now, Roger, you're not taking him back to Miss Monroe's house, are you?' said Tony severely. 'That would be very much frowned on indeed.'

'Definitely not,' said Roger. 'I'm not here to take Colin back to Miss Monroe's house. I promise you that.'

'Oh well, that's all right, then. Just for a moment I thought she might have sent you over to collect him.'

'No,' said Roger. 'No, she didn't. Colin, why don't you hop in? It's time we were off.'

'Where to, Roger?' I asked, climbing into the front seat. 'Where on earth are we going?'

'Never you mind. Just shut the door, would you?' He scrunched the Wolsey into first gear.

Tony peered nosily through the rear window, but we were already on the move.

'Wait a minute! What's under that rug in the back seat? I thought I saw it move.'

'That's my little dog, sir,' said Roger over his shoulder. We're going to take her for a walk in Windsor Great Park.'

We lurched off round the corner of the drive, leaving Tony standing on the lawn scratching his head.

'Why have you left Miss Monroe alone, Roger?' I asked. 'I thought I told you never to do so.'

'Surpri-hise!'

Marilyn's blonde head suddenly erupted in the rear-view mirror like a jack-in-a-box, giving me partial heart failure.

'Marilyn! What on earth are you doing here?'

Peals of giggles. 'Well, that's better. It's "Marilyn" at last. I'm fed up with that "Miss Monroe" stuff. It sounds so pompous. And anyway, I don't want to be Miss Monroe today. I just want to be me. Roger and I thought we'd come over and give you a surprise. Aren't you pleased to see me?'

'Of course, I'm thrilled to bits. It's just that yesterday, er, everyone seemed very cross that I'd gone over to Parkside at all, and that I was interfering with your life and the film and all that.'

'Oh, nonsense,' said Marilyn. 'Don't you take any notice of those old spoilsports. It's a lovely summer day, and Roger and I decided to go out for an adventure, didn't we, Roger?'

'Hmm,' said Roger. He slowed the car to a halt, with two wheels on the grass verge. 'Now, where are we going?'

I swivelled round and stared into Marilyn's very naughty eyes.

'Yes, but Milton said that if I ever spoke to you again he would have me sacked and banned from the studio.'

Marilyn frowned. 'I used to have another coach before Paula. You wouldn't believe how often she was banned from the set. But she never went. No one can sack you, Colin – except me, of course.' Another giggle. 'You're quite safe.'

'What the . . . ?'

Unheard by us, Tony had come padding down the drive to investigate, and was now staring into the back seat, his face contorted with rage.

Marilyn screamed and buried herself under the rug. Roger let out the clutch with a jolt, and the car flapped off again like an old black crow.

'Wait!' shouted Tony. 'Colin! I want a word with you!' But this time Roger's police training stood him in good stead. No one was going to kidnap Marilyn Monroe while he was at the wheel, not even Mr Bushell.

'Phew! That was a close one.' Marilyn emerged from the rug looking even more dishevelled and cheeky than before. 'Do you think he saw me?'

'I'm quite sure he did,' I said. 'He'll be on the phone to Sir Laurence already.'

'Ooh. What do you think Sir Laurence will say?'

'He'll think it over for a minute, and then he'll laugh out loud and tell Tony not to tell anyone else, to keep it a secret.'

'You know Sir Laurence pretty well, don't you, Colin?'

'Yes, I do, and he's a great man. But I realise that he probably doesn't look like one to you at the moment.'

'Oh, I don't know about that. He's just so terribly severe. He treats me like a schoolgirl, not an actress.'

'That's just his manner. He can see you're an actress every time he looks at the previous day's film. We all can.'

'I hate to interrupt,' said Roger, 'but where are we going?'

'Anywhere,' said Marilyn. 'It's Saturday, and I want to be free. How about that Windsor Park you mentioned to Mr Bushell? Do you think he'll follow us and spy? Hey, it doesn't matter. We've got Roger. We can go wherever we want.'

'Windsor Great Park it is, then,' said Roger. A few minutes later he swung the car down a long avenue of trees. 'It's right here.'

Soon we reached a pair of tall iron gates with a little gatehouse beside them. Roger stopped, got out and knocked. A man came to the door and Roger chatted to him for a few moments, then showed him what I presume was some sort of pass.

'I don't like being on my own in the back,' said Marilyn. 'I feel like the Queen. Come and join me.' I squashed into the Wolsey's less than commodious rear seat beside her. 'That's it. You said you weren't scared of me. Snuggle up. This is fun.'

Roger got back behind the wheel, and sighed at the now vacant front seat beside him as the man opened the gates.

'We're off to see Her Majesty now,' he said. 'You two just behave yourselves in the back seat.'

'Ooh,' said Marilyn, 'Mr Bushell can't follow us here.' And she gave my arm a squeeze.

This was all going much too fast for me. I felt as if I was the one who had been kidnapped. I mean, it was incredibly exhilarating to be in the back seat of a smelly black Wolsey with Marilyn Monroe, speeding through the back entrance to Windsor Castle – but what would happen next? I wasn't even wearing a jacket. Where could we go? What could I do? After this, how could I go back to working on the film as third assistant director? All the normal, everyday rules seemed to have been chucked out of the window. Roger was the only sensible person in Marilyn's whole entourage, and now he seemed to be in on some sort of plot. I could probably be sued for breach of contract, or alienation of affection, or something. Maybe the studio would have me bumped off. I was responsible, they would say, for the abduction of their million-dollar film star, the most famous woman in the world. What if we crashed and she was killed?

'Stop the car, Roger,' I said. 'Let's get out and think. There's no one around. Let's have a little stroll in the fresh air.'

Roger drew in to the side of the road and Marilyn and I got out. She still had hold of my arm, I noticed.

'I'll stay here on guard,' said Roger. 'Why don't you two walk down to that little stream and cool off?'

'Great idea,' said Marilyn, releasing her grip and bending down to pull off her shoes. She was wearing a short white wool dress instead of her usual trousers, and she presented, as she must well have been aware, an extremely attractive rear end.

'Come on, Colin.' She swayed off down the slope, her bare feet crinkling the grass. 'Don't be stuffy. Take your shoes off. It's great.'

By the time we reached the stream, we were out of breath and very hot, and it seemed a good idea to wade straight in. 'I think this is the most lovely thing I've ever felt in my life,' said Marilyn, serious at last. 'What do you think, Colin? Can't you feel it?' She held out both her hands and grasped mine. 'I feel so alive. For the first time I feel like I was part of nature. Can't you feel it, Colin? I'm sure you can feel it too.'

Frankly, I felt as if I was going to drown, although the water was only two inches deep.

'I can feel it, Marilyn,' I mumbled.

But she wasn't listening to me.

'Why do I take all those pills? Why do I worry about what all those men think? Why do I let myself get pushed around? This is how I ought to feel, every day of my life. This is the real me . . . isn't it, Colin?'

My feet had grown cold by now, and I led her to the bank and sat down.

'No, Marilyn. Alas, it's not the real you. It's just a beautiful, beautiful illusion. You are a star. A great star.' I was beginning to sound like Paula Strasberg, but it was true. 'You can't escape that. You have to perform. Millions of people love you and admire you. You can't ignore them. You can't run away. Let's just have a super fun day, a day that we will never forget, and then we must go back to real life.'

'Only one day?'

'Well . . . perhaps a weekend?'

'Or a week?'

'We'll see.'

Marilyn brightened. 'OK. So how shall we spend our day?'

'Let's go to Windsor Castle. Her Majesty might be in. Then we could go across to my old school, Eton College. There's a little tea shop where they give you the most scrumptious food. Then maybe we could have a swim in the river before we go home.'

'That sounds great. Let's go. Do you think Roger will mind if we treat him like a chauffeur?'

I gazed into her eyes. 'He'd do anything for you, Marilyn, as you know.'

Roger obviously knew the road to Windsor Castle well. 'I used to work here,' he said. 'Looking after the Family.'

He parked on the slope leading to the main gate and marched up to the guardhouse, with Marilyn and me a few steps behind. He was obviously glad to be back in charge.

There were two large uniformed policemen blocking the archway, and although they did not know Roger personally, it was quite clear that like recognised like at about twenty feet.

'Detective Chief Superintendent Smith,' said Roger. 'I'm escorting this lady and gentleman for the day, and they wish to see round the castle. Is there any way in which you can assist?'

'Do they know anyone here, sir? We need to write down a contact name in the book. Otherwise one of us would need to be with them at all times, and they might not want that, sir.'

Marilyn was clutching my hand in a rather desperate fashion, and I sensed that she was scared stiff that they would recognise her – and at the same time terrified that they would not.

'My godfather works here,' I said. 'I used to visit him quite often when I was at school. He's the librarian. He's called Sir Owen Morshead. Maybe you could call him.'

Eyebrows shot up all round. I was wearing a white shirt, grey flannel trousers and sandals, not exactly the dress of a typical castle visitor. We all went inside the guardhouse, and the policeman dialled a number.

'Sir Owen? Main gate here, sir. I have a young gentleman, name of –? '

'Clark. Colin Clark.'

'Name of Clark here, sir, would like a word with you, sir.' He handed the phone to me.

'Colin, is that you? What are you doing here?' Owen Morshead is an eccentric scholar with a wonderful sense of humour. He has an equally delightful wife called Paquita, and together they are like a breath of fresh air in royal circles.

'I'm working on a film nearby, and I thought I would

bring my, er, friend, my lady friend' – I grinned at Marilyn
– 'over for you to meet her.'

'How delightful,' said Owen. 'I'm expecting some visitors
in a short time, so it would be nice if you could come right
now. Do bring her up at once. Just follow the road up the
hill until you see another policeman outside my door. He'll
direct you.'

'I think I'll just wait at the gate,' said Roger. 'You'll be
safe enough in the castle, Miss Monroe.'

'Ssh!' said Marilyn with a broad wink and a wiggle,
which made the two policemen's eyes pop out, and off
we set.

News spreads fast, and at the next police post three or
four men came tumbling out to see if it was true. In fact
they were so intent on gazing at my 'lady friend' that I had
to push them out of the way so that we could get through
the library door.

Once inside we were in another world. Sir Owen Morshead did not look as if he had ever been to the cinema in
his life.

'How charming, how charming. You are pretty, my dear.
I'm sure you and Colin have so much in common. Well,
this is my humble den.' His arm swept round the Royal
Library, room after room lined with books and pictures.
The tables were covered with books, all the chairs had books
piled on top of them, and there were even stacks of books
on the floor.

Owen gave a hoot of laughter. 'It looks rather dull and
dusty, doesn't it?' he said, but Marilyn was in awe.

'Oh, Sir Owen' – you never quite knew whether she

would remember a name or not – 'I love books,' she said in a childlike whisper. 'Have you read them all?'

'Luckily one doesn't have to do that.' Owen was enjoying himself immensely. 'A lot of them just have pictures.' He took a large portfolio from a shelf and opened it. 'These are all by an artist called Holbein.'

'Ooh, what a beautiful lady,' said Marilyn, looking over his shoulder. 'Who is she?'

'She was the daughter of one of the King's courtiers, four hundred years ago.'

'Imagine, four hundred years ago, and she still looks great. Gee. How many of these have you got?'

'Eighty-nine. And these,' said Owen, taking out another folder of drawings, 'are all by an Italian artist called Leonardo da Vinci.'

'Wait a minute!' cried Marilyn. 'I've heard of him.' You never knew with Marilyn. 'Didn't he paint that picture of the lady with the funny smile? You know the one I mean, Colin.'

'The *Mona Lisa.*'

'Yeah, that's her. Have you got that here too?'

'Alas, no,' said Owen, sighing. 'That one got away. But enough of all this art. I mustn't bore you with my hobby.'

'You aren't boring me, Sir Owen,' whispered Marilyn. 'I love it here. I could sit here for hours.'

'Let's go and look at the part of the castle where the Queen lives. She's not here at the moment, but she will be very sorry to have missed you.'

'Really?' said Marilyn in total amazement.

'Oh, yes,' said Owen. 'Why, she was only saying to me

the other day, what must it be like to be the most famous woman in the world?'

So, you could never tell with Owen either.

'Now this,' he went on 'is the White Drawing Room. Very pretty, isn't it? And that is a portrait of King George the Third. He was the one who was silly enough to lose our American colonies two hundred years ago. And that is his wife, and those are his children.'

'Oh, they're gorgeous,' said Marilyn, completely unable to figure out whether Owen had recognised her or not.

We were almost having to run in order to keep up with him as he strode through one huge chamber after another.

'And this the Green Drawing Room. A lovely view of Windsor Great Park out of the windows, isn't it? But you've been there already, haven't you?'

That gatekeeper had probably telephoned him and warned him of our arrival – like all royal courtiers, Owen had a network of spies.

'And this is the Crimson Drawing Room. It is a little opulent, I suppose.' Even Owen could not resist showing off. There weren't many rival monarchs left to impress, but Hollywood film stars were the next best thing.

Marilyn was stunned. 'You mean Her Majesty actually lives here, in these rooms?!'

'Well, she has her own private apartment where she sleeps, but this is where she entertains.'

'Gee!' said Marilyn.

'If it all seems a little overwhelming,' said Owen with great glee, 'let's look at something a little smaller.' He led

Marilyn photographed by Jack
Cardiff, the lighting cameraman
on *The Prince and the Showgirl*, in
1956, shortly after the events
described in this book.

Marilyn loved Jack Cardiff. He was an artist who recognised her tragic side, seeing her as a Renoir girl, rather than as a sex symbol. These pictures (like others in this book, none of which has been published before) are from a very happy photo session Marilyn had with Jack Cardiff at Parkside House.

Marilyn turned up late for the London first night of her new husband Arthur Miller's *A View from the Bridge* during the filming of *The Prince and the Showgirl*, and stole the show by wearing a very revealing red dress.

Marilyn with Olivier on the set of
The Prince and the Showgirl. This
publicity still by the film's producer,
Milton Greene, hints at the mistrust
the pair felt for each other.

Myself at the age of twenty-three. I was given the job of third assistant director on *The Prince and the Showgirl* because my parents were friends of Laurence Olivier.

Milton Greene was a brilliant photographer who was to experience many difficulties during the shooting of *The Prince and the Showgirl*, his first film as producer.

Marilyn always loved being photographed, and Jack Cardiff was one of
the few Englishmen whom she trusted to do her justice.

Marilyn on the lot for the coronation scene, being attended to by hairdresser Gordon Bond, under the eye of Jack Cardiff.

Olivier was always more relaxed when Marilyn was not on the set. Here he tries to teach Jeremy Spenser, who played the young King, to slide down the banister. (He failed, and the scene was not included in the film.)

Marilyn poses a problem to Richard Wattis (who played Mr Northbrook of the Foreign Office), Olivier, Jack Cardiff and camera operator Denys Coop.

Marilyn as chorus girl Elsie Marina with her friend Fanny, played by Daphne Anderson, in their digs.

us along a very wide, grand corridor lined with pictures, then through a small door, and down a staircase.

'Now, what do you think of this?' We were in a plain stone room, completely filled by an enormous dolls' house furnished and decorated like a tiny mansion. Everything imaginable was inside – beds, chairs, baths, basins, taps, table lamps, rugs, chandeliers, all accurate down to the tiniest detail, and all exactly to scale. There were cars in the garage, lawnmowers on the grass, pots and pans and food in the kitchen, even a little Singer sewing machine on the nursery table.

Marilyn clasped her hands in rapture and dropped to her knees. She looked so young and so innocent that my heart nearly broke. Owen, too, did not take his eyes off her as for nearly a minute she simply radiated joy. Then she stood up, squared her shoulders and looked straight ahead. 'I sure never had a dolls' house like that when I was a kid. Why, most people I knew didn't even have a house that size. But I guess if you're a queen . . .'

'And now I'm sure you must be longing to get on your way,' Owen said. One of the first things a courtier learns is how to stop guests staying for too long. 'But I'll tell Her Majesty you were here. I believe you are due to meet her next month.' (She was, at the Royal premiere of the film *The Battle of the River Plate*.)

'So you do know who I am,' said Marilyn.

'Of course I do, dear girl. And I'm very flattered that my godson brought you to see me. You're every bit as lovely as your photographs.' This wasn't quite true at that moment, I thought. Marilyn looked like a waif. 'Now, goodbye, goodbye. I mustn't keep you,' and we were popped out of another little door, into the sunshine.

'Wow!' said Marilyn. 'You've got quite a godfather, Colin. Do you think he's like that with the Queen?'

'Identical,' I said. 'That's why she likes him.'

When we got back to the main gate, a crowd had gathered. Despite Roger's protests, the two policemen had told their friends who the visitor was, and they had told their friends, etc. At first I thought Marilyn would be nervous, but she was clearly thrilled. She must have been feeling a bit unhappy at being incognito to her public for so long.

'Shall I be "*her*"?' she asked.

Without waiting for an answer, she jumped up on a step and struck a pose. Her hip went out, her shoulders went back, her famous bosom was thrust forward. She pouted her lips and opened her eyes very wide, and there, suddenly, was the image the whole world knew. Instinctively the audience started to applaud. Several of them had cameras, and for a few minutes Marilyn gave them all the poses they required. Considering that she had hardly any make-up on, and had not done her hair, it was an incredible performance.

But I felt distinctly uneasy. What was I doing with this Hollywood star? A moment ago I had been squeezing her hand as if she was a girlfriend. If I didn't watch out, I was going to make a complete fool of myself. I would never have dared to take liberties like that with Vivien Leigh – and I knew her much better than Marilyn, who I hardly knew at all. I found myself skulking at the edge of the group, feeling about two feet tall and wishing I was dead.

Finally Roger decided the crowd was getting too big, and gave a signal to the policemen. They pushed the onlookers to one side and made a path for us, although people were still frantically pushing forward to catch another glimpse, as if some goddess had come down from heaven into their midst.

'Who are you?' One man challenged me as I tried to squeeze into the back of the car.

'Oh, I'm no one,' I said. 'I'm just working on the film with Miss Monroe.'

'You must never say you're no one,' said Marilyn very seriously when the door had shut. 'You are *you*. Anyway, it's me who should be asking that question. Who do I think I am? Marilyn Monroe?' And she burst into giggles. 'I'm hungry, Colin. Where are we going to eat?'

We went to an olde-worlde tea shop in Eton High Street called The Cockpit, all black beams and inglenook fireplaces and little old ladies eating scones. I had thought of going to the Old House Hotel, which has excellent food, but someone would certainly have recognised Marilyn, and I couldn't face that again. I had just been reminded how quickly Marilyn could attract a crowd. I suppose I was getting possessive – and the truth was that I preferred being with Marilyn when she was frail, and not playing the great star. Now she looked like a schoolgirl as she tucked into a large pile of egg and cress sandwiches, and sipped coffee out of a mug. My heart went out to her again.

'What are we going to do next, Colin? I haven't felt so hungry in ages. Boy, these sandwiches are really good. Pretty fattening too, I guess, but what the heck. I feel as if I was being taken out on a treat. Did you ever get taken here by your mom and dad? Now I can imagine exactly how you felt.'

'Let's go and have a look at my school,' I said. 'I haven't been back there since I was eighteen.'

'That long, huh? But don't forget about the swim. You promised a swim.'

'We haven't got any swimming costumes,' I protested. (Just imagine what a crowd that could involve. There'd be a riot.)

'Oh, phooey,' said Marilyn. 'You can wear your pants. After all, it isn't every day that you get a chance to go swimming with Marilyn Monroe.' She hooted with giggles again, making the old ladies at the nearby tables give us disapproving looks.

'Roger,' I said, 'there's a clothes shop across the road. Could you pop across and buy a couple of towels and a pair of swimming trunks for me? I'll pay you back for all this when we get home.'

'If we get home in one piece,' muttered Roger. He clearly thought that swimming was a very bad idea, but he went anyway, coming back into the tea shop a few minutes later with a brown paper parcel which he put disapprovingly under his seat.

'This is such fun,' said Marilyn. 'I'm so excited. Let's go.'

'A bit more culture first,' I said. 'It will warm us up.'

'Ooh,' said Marilyn.

Roger drove us off, and stopped by Eton School yard. We all went inside.

'It all looks awfully old,' said Marilyn. 'And a little bit dusty too, if I may say so.'

'It is old,' I said. 'Over five hundred years. That statue is of the founder of the school, King Henry the Sixth. When we were students, if we didn't work hard enough we would be beaten with a bundle of sticks. It was called being swiped, and it took place in that room over there. Our trousers would be pulled down, and we would be whipped until the blood ran down our legs. The legend was that if a boy could break away, climb the railings and touch the foot of the statue before he was caught he would get the royal pardon, and wouldn't be swiped.'

'Gosh. I'm not sure I like this nobility stuff. Were you ever beaten, Colin?'

'I was beaten quite often with a cane, Marilyn, but I was never swiped.'

'Poor Colin. I had a very unhappy time as a kid, but I was never beaten like that. Let's get out of here before they catch us. Race you back to the car,' and she ran off across the quadrangle like a gazelle, with me in pursuit.

The day had become hot and sultry. Roger had left the car in the shade, but the temperature in the back of the old Wolsey was now tropical. I showed Roger where to turn off the main road in order to get within a reasonable distance of the river. The track was more bumpy than I remembered, and Marilyn held on to me for dear life, so by the time the car stopped, we were glued together with perspiration. It was with huge relief that we dashed across the grass to the water's edge and prepared to plunge in.

'This is the only place where there's sand to walk on,' I

said. 'That's why it's the nicest place for a dip. I've swum here many, many times, even at the risk of being beaten. But watch out, Marilyn. The water's cold.'

'That's just what I need!' cried Marilyn. 'A cold bath. But why isn't there anyone else here?'

'All the boys have gone home for the summer holidays.'

I take a long time to get undressed (or dressed, for that matter). For some reason, I always think I have to be neat. By the time I had got my new trunks on, Marilyn and I having taken separate bushes behind which to change, I had already heard the splash of Marilyn jumping into the water. When I finally emerged, her smiling blonde head was bobbing about on the surface of the Thames. As I waded in to join her, I could hear her singing to herself, and laughing out loud.

'Oh, I'm so happy. I really feel that this is happening to me, and no one else.' She stared at me, laughed again, stared again, and then suddenly looked serious. 'Colin,' she called, 'I've got something in my eye. Would you help me get it out?'

Laboriously I waded towards her through the icy water, my hands held high above my head, and peered down into her huge eyes. Marilyn put out her arms, clasped them behind my head, pulled my head to hers and kissed me full on the lips.

It took about a hundredth of a second before I realised what was going on, and then another hundredth before I realised that Marilyn was naked, at least from the waist up. The sensation of her lips and bosom pressed against mine, combined with the icy water, nearly caused me to pass out.

'Phew! That was great,' gasped Marilyn. 'That's the first time I've ever kissed anyone younger than me. Shall we do it again?'

'Later, Marilyn darling.' I was in a panic. 'What if a boat comes past? And anyway, we'll freeze. You wait here for a second while I get the towels. If you come out like that and someone sees you, we'll get arrested.'

'Oh, nonsense,' said Marilyn, wading out with me. 'Roger will fix it. Now, Colin, it's nothing you haven't seen before.'

It was true that I had indeed once seen her in the nude when I accidentally barged into her dressing room unannounced, but that did not mean that I could keep my eyes off her now. Her beautiful body was simply glowing with health and vitality, and she reminded me of one of those adorable young ladies who sit on clouds in paintings by Tiepolo. I reached the bank before her, grabbed one of the towels and wrapped it round as much of her as I could. Then I picked up the other one to hide the all too obvious evidence of the powerful attraction which I felt.

'Oh, Colin,' giggled Marilyn. 'And you an old Etonian.' She threw back her head and laughed, because that was what she had said when I had burst in on her before, and she knew it had caught me out. 'That was great. I'm not used to being kissed, you know. The men in my life don't seem to have time. They either jump straight on top of me, or want me to jump straight on top of them.'

Roger was sleeping peacefully under a tree when we got back to the car, and he viewed our tousled appearance and wet clothes with obvious disapproval. 'Time to go home, I'd say.'

'I suppose it is,' said Marilyn. Suddenly she looked depressed. She got into the car and hunched down in the back seat, like a child who knows it is going to be punished.

The drive back to Parkside House took twenty minutes. I held her hand, but she didn't speak again. For some reason I felt desperately guilty, but there was nothing I could say. It was time to be grown up again.

Sure enough, when we arrived there were two cars parked in the drive, and when we went in, two men waiting in the hall. One was Milton Greene. The other was Marilyn's lawyer, Irving Stein.

'Hello, Irving. Hello, Milt,' said Marilyn sweetly. 'Roger can drive you home now, Colin. And if you' – looking at her lawyer and her co-producer – 'hurt one hair of his head, or get him fired off this picture, I'll be very, very upset. Understand?'

'Yes, Marilyn,' they both gulped.

'*Very* upset.' And she vanished upstairs.

'Perhaps we could just have a word with you, Mr Clark, before you leave,' said Stein.

'I suppose so,' I said warily. They looked like the enemy to me.

'Have you heard of the legal term "enticement"? Miss Monroe is legally contracted to us, as you know. Anyone who entices her not to fulfil her contractual obligations to us could be held responsible under the law. And this includes her personal relationships.'

Milton looked wretched, like one of the Lost Boys in *Peter Pan*, but Stein was clearly in charge.

'Every single minute that I have spent with Miss Monroe

has been at her invitation,' I replied. 'And what is more, we have never been out of the presence of Detective Chief Superintendent Roger Smith of Scotland Yard. You could hardly ask for a more reliable chaperone than that. Catch you later, Milton. Come on, Roger, I thought you were going to give me a lift. Mustn't keep you waiting . . .' And I was gone.

I asked Roger to drop me at the pub near Runnymede House, and I had dinner there. I could not face explaining what had happened to anyone. Tony would most definitely not have understood.

When I did get to bed, I could not sleep. The image of Marilyn seemed to be dancing round my head – laughing, weeping, waving, sighing – twice lifesize. I remembered the kiss, but I couldn't seem to remember feeling it. I was immensely exhilarated, but at the same time desperately sad. When I did finally pass out, I dreamed that I was swimming in a stormy sea, towards a life raft that I could see and even feel, but never quite grasp.

'Well, well. Who's been a naughty boy, then?'

Next morning, at Runnymede House, Anne Bushell was positively flirtatious. 'Tony nearly had an apoplectic fit when he saw Marilyn in the back of Roger's car.'

'Me too.'

'Oh, so you didn't know she was going to be there? It wasn't all a cunning plot?'

'If it was, I wasn't in on it, I can assure you. It was just a sudden whim of Marilyn's. She wanted to escape that stuffy house, and all those people telling her what to do. She can be tremendous fun, you know.'

'I'll bet she can,' said Anne.

I ignored the innuendo.

'What did you two do together, exactly?'

'We went to Windsor Castle and met my godfather – he's the Royal Librarian. We had lunch at a tea shop and then we visited Eton College.'

'That all sounds very nice and cultural, but it doesn't quite explain your appearance when you got in last night.'

I had gone straight up to my room, but Anne always noticed everything.

'You looked as if you'd been swimming to me. Can Marilyn swim?'

'Well, er . . . yes, she can, actually, very well, and you see, it was so frightfully hot, so we went for a dip in the river at a little spot I knew from when I was a schoolboy.'

'Quite,' said Anne. 'I'd better not ask what you used for swimming costumes.'

I was temporarily saved from this line of questioning by the telephone ringing in the hall.

Predictably, it was Milton Greene. 'Hey, Colin, I wonder if I could drop over for a chat. Everything's fine. Don't worry, I'm not going to scold you. I just think we should talk – man to man.'

'Anne, is it all right if Milton comes over? . . . OK, Milton,' I said wearily. 'Come over, but Anne's going to give us lunch at one o'clock, so you'll have to be gone by then.'

'Take him out into the garden,' said Anne after I'd hung up. 'Perhaps the English countryside will help him to calm down.'

Ten minutes later, Milton drove up.

'Let's walk down to the river's edge,' I said. 'This place is called Runnymede. Do you know why Runnymede is famous?'

'No,' said Milton.

'Runnymede is the island on the River Thames where King John was forced to sign the Magna Carta on 15 June 1215. Every English schoolboy knows that. That's 741 years ago, Milton, and the Magna Carta is still the foundation of the British Constitution today. Among other things, it guaranteed every man the right to a fair trial. The barons had to capture London before the King would agree to sign it. I only mention this because I want to put my little trip with Marilyn into perspective.'

'Hey, Colin, I'm not mad at you. Not mad at all. I've just come over to give you a word of advice. I'm entirely on your side. I just don't want you to get hurt, that's all.'

Oh, sure, I thought. Except you wouldn't mind if I broke every bone in my body falling off a cliff.

'How kind of you, Milton.'

'You see, I've known Marilyn for a very long time – it must be seven years now – and I understand where she's coming from. I fell in love with her just like you did. She was living with a powerful Hollywood agent called Johnny Hyde and I was a photographer for *Life* magazine, and she and I had a ten-day romance. That's the trouble with Marilyn, and there's no way I can break this to you gently, Colin. Marilyn has a romance with anybody who happens to take her fancy. I know you put her on a pedestal. We all do. But it's a mistake to fall in love with her. She'll only break your heart. You've obviously had a great time together. Now leave it at that. Get out before you get burned.'

'Finished, Milton?'

'Hey, don't get mad. I'm sorry I had to tell you this, but it's for your own good.'

'Firstly,' I said, 'Marilyn may have "a romance", as you put it, with the man in the moon for all I care, but she isn't having one with me. It is possible to spend the day together and have a lot of fun without romance, you know.'

Milton looked doubtful. 'She said you kissed her.'

'Secondly, I have not fallen in love with Marilyn. I don't know about Hollywood, but in England we take a little longer than a day to fall in love. And thirdly, I have not put Marilyn on a pedestal, or anywhere else. To me she is just a beautiful, funny, rather sad lady whose company I enjoy enormously. Of course I realise that she's also the most famous film star in the world. Nor have I forgotten that she's on her honeymoon, and that her husband is a well-known writer. But she is under tremendous pressure. She's trying to give a great performance in a very difficult film. Her co-star is being horrid to her. She doesn't know who she can trust.'

Milton frowned.

'Now her husband has left her for ten days, I can't imagine why. So she jolly well deserves a day off, and if she chooses to spend it with me, I just count myself incredibly lucky, and I certainly won't refuse.'

'Did she say anything about me? Or the filming?'

'Nothing. Not a word. She did not utter one word of complaint the whole day. We went to see my godfather . . .'

'Yeah, I heard. Gee, I'd sure like to see those pictures. Those Holbein drawings are probably the greatest portraits in the world. I'm a portrait photographer, don't forget.'

'Maybe we can go over there one day. Then Marilyn and I went out to lunch – always with Roger by our side – and then we went to look at my old school. Marilyn was more interested in culture than romance.'

'And then you went for a swim. She said you went for a swim, and kissed in the water.'

Poor Marilyn, I thought. She's like a little girl. Why does she tell Milton everything, as if he was her father? 'Daddy, Daddy, I kissed Colin.' She's trying to rebel, I suppose.

'Well, she's home now,' I said, 'safe and sound. Perhaps a little fresh air and exercise will have done her good. I hope Sir Laurence realises that I've been working hard for him all weekend. We've still got a film to make.'

'Marilyn had forgotten that she'd promised to go over her lines with Paula Strasberg this afternoon, so they're doing that now. Paula said Marilyn was very nervous, and asked for some pills.'

'Pills? What the hell does she need pills for?'

'Colin, you don't understand.'

'I understand, all right. She's scared – of Paula and you, as well as Olivier. You're all meant to be working with her, not against her. And I think she's hooked on those pills. She can never be herself. None of you want her to be herself. You want her to be "Marilyn Monroe, Hollywood sex goddess", because that's where the money is. Just imagine how difficult it is for her. Even in the movie, she can't be "Elsie Marina, the showgirl" – she has to be "Marilyn Monroe, the Hollywood sex goddess, acting Elsie Marina, the showgirl". That's why she has such difficulty with her part, and can't remember her lines. Underneath it all she's just a lonely, simple child, who deserves to be happy, just like any child. But you lot stretch her until she's about to break. And one day she will break, and where will you be then? Long gone, and making a fuss of someone else, I'll bet.'

'Hey – so you are in love with her, Colin!'

I could only groan.

To do him justice, Milton seemed genuinely upset by my attack on his motives. He paced up and down that beautiful island on the Thames just as King John must have paced over seven hundred years ago, and told me the whole history of his relationship with Marilyn. After their short affair they had become friends. Marilyn was a victim of the old studio system, whereby actors got trapped in long-term contracts from which they could never escape, no matter how famous they became. The studios would dictate the roles they played, ruthlessly typecasting them to exploit their fame. The studios squeezed every possible dollar out of their films, while still paying the star the tiny salary they had originally signed for. Milton had persuaded Marilyn to rebel. By clever manipulation, and with the help of his lawyer friend Irving Stein, Milton had enabled Marilyn to escape from her contract with Twentieth Century-Fox, and to ensure that when she re-signed it – not even Marilyn, it seems, can operate without a contract – it was on much better terms. From then on Marilyn could decide which films she did or didn't make, and even make a film entirely on her own. *The Prince and the Showgirl* was the first film being made by Marilyn Monroe Productions, of which Milton was an equal partner.

'Well, not quite equal, Colin,' Milton admitted. 'Fifty-one per cent to her, and 49 per cent to me. But heck, 49 per cent of Marilyn Monroe can't be bad, can it?'

'I'd like 1 per cent,' I said.

Milton grinned ruefully.

'Marilyn's hard to pin down. It's like owning 49 per cent

of a dream. It doesn't mean very much. I think you do own 1 per cent of her right now, Colin, and it's probably worth more than my 49 per cent. The trouble is, for how long?'

Milton suddenly sat down on the grass and put his head in his hands. 'I'm not sure I can go on for much longer, but I've got no choice. I've got every single penny I ever earned invested in Marilyn, and she simply doesn't understand what that means. I've been paying her living expenses for over a year now – her apartment, her staff, her shopping, her doctors – it adds up to thousands of dollars. Twentieth Century-Fox won't release any money until she starts working for them again, so I have to pay. Don't get me wrong. Marilyn doesn't ask for lots of cash; she just never gives it a thought. She's not interested in money, actually. She's only interested in her career. But she loves to be generous, and that can cost a lot. And Arthur needs money, and Lee Strasberg needs money, and they both treat Marilyn like a bank. Now, Warner Brothers have put up the cash for this film, but when I start taking some of my investment back, Marilyn thinks I'm swindling her. I'm sure she's been put up to that by Arthur. He's definitely not on my side, Colin. He's looking out for himself. But Marilyn worships him, you know.'

'I certainly don't worship him,' I said. 'I think he's too vain. I don't think he loves Marilyn as much as she thinks, either. Not in the way she deserves to be loved, anyway.'

'You're right. He's a bigger damn prima donna than she is. Now he's behaving like he'd had some awful surprise.

He must already have known what life with Marilyn would be like. When he first met her she was Elia Kazan's mistress, and she was very mixed up. Then he saw her when she was filming *Bus Stop* with Josh Logan. She'd phone him for hours on end, and it can't have been hard to see how nervous she got when she had to give a performance. I think he just liked the image of himself as the man who captured the most famous woman in the world. It made him as famous as her. He wants to control her, and that makes him try to turn her against me. And now he's gone running off to Paris, and from there he's going to New York, as if he was fed up with Marilyn after only four weeks. I'd much rather Marilyn ran off with you, believe me.'

'Me too. But that's not going to happen, Milton, I can assure you, so you can relax.'

'Paula's after Marilyn's money too. Well, it's not really Paula, it's Lee. Paula is a very unstable lady – which is sort of a pity, since Marilyn depends on her for her stability. Paula's a frustrated actress. She has no self-confidence at all. She pours all her hopes and fears into Marilyn – like a typical Jewish mother, I suppose. That feeds into Marilyn's insecurity, and Lee takes advantage of it. Lee wants to be a great impresario, and Marilyn is his passport to the fame he thinks he deserves. He's charging a fortune for Paula to be here. More than anyone else. Much more than me. Why is everybody in the film business a frustrated something or other, who thinks they deserve to be paid thousands of dollars a week?'

'I don't think Olivier is that frustrated,' I said. 'Except

perhaps in bed. And I don't think he's that interested in money, either.'

'No, basically Olivier is one of the good guys. He's just out of his depth. He doesn't have any idea what's going on in Marilyn's head. He treats her like a silly little blonde, even though he can see in the dailies that she's really very good – better than he is, I'd say. Olivier is an old-fashioned actor with a great reputation. Marilyn thought that if she acted with him she'd be taken seriously at last. That's why she wanted to buy the rights to *The Sleeping Prince* – so she could tempt Olivier with a script she knew he liked. After all, he'd done it on stage, and with his wife. Imagine if little Marilyn could steal a part from the great Vivien Leigh, and maybe seduce Laurence Olivier as well. I must admit I thought she was crazy, but she brought it off – almost.'

'Poor Marilyn. She must be disappointed. She couldn't seduce Olivier, so she ended up with me.'

'You're making her happy right now, Colin. But, as I said, for how long? Nobody makes Marilyn happy for very long, and that's the truth.'

At one o'clock Tony came to tell me that lunch was ready, and Milton left. Tony was in a terrible sulk, so it was an uncomfortable meal. I felt sad that I had disobeyed his orders, especially as I was a guest in his home, but I had no regrets. Looking back on it, Saturday had been the happiest day of my life.

Monday, 17 September

Back in the studio on Monday morning, things were even more depressing than usual. Marilyn didn't show up, and when I called the house as usual at nine a.m., Roger could tell me nothing. She was still in bed. He didn't know why. I was sure she had taken too many pills. Milton and Paula were regaining control. They would rather have a beautiful corpse than a free spirit, I said to myself, gnashing my teeth; but there was absolutely nothing I could do. I had served my purpose and been dismissed.

Milton turned up at the studio at eleven o'clock, and went straight into conference with Olivier. He looked grim and tired, and I don't suppose any conclusion was reached. I was convinced that the crew must be thinking of me as an upstart, someone who had had the cheek to fly too high, and had got his wings burned as a result. But I could not take my mind off what might be going on at Parkside House. Marilyn was certainly dreadfully confused, and probably desperately unhappy. I knew she liked to work, if she could. She wanted to finish the film. What could she be doing all afternoon? That house was like a prison, like an asylum. I should never have let her go back there. By lunchtime, I was really worried.

'Colin is really worried!'

Dicky Wattis always seemed to know exactly what I was thinking. He is old – at least he seems old to me* – and thin and very perspicacious. 'Frankly, my dear, I couldn't care less if Marilyn Monroe dropped dead,' he said sniffily. 'She's giving the rest of us actors a simply dreadful time, keeping us waiting for hours in these stuffy costumes.' Dicky had to wear a uniform with gold braid up to his throat. The only things he seemed to like were the white silk stockings and patent leather slippers that went with it. 'If the film can't be finished, the insurance company will pay us off and we can all go home.'

'She's trying her best, Dicky,' I said. It was dangerous to show any support for Marilyn on that set, but I couldn't resist it. Thank goodness, no one seemed to know about our excursion on Saturday. Olivier must have sworn Tony to secrecy, because he had been literally bursting to tell someone last night.

'It's all those people around her,' I went on. 'Roger tells me she was fine yesterday. They scare her to death, and then she thinks she needs those pills.'

'She's Marilyn Monroe, dear,' said Dicky. 'That's her life. Pills, booze, sex, publicity. What a way to carry on. I only wish I could be the same.'

'Oh, Dicky. How can you say that? She's really very confused. It's like the script of this film. She doesn't have enough love in her life.'

---

* He was forty-three.

'Nor do I, dear,' said Dicky, laughing. 'Nor do we all. Don't you worry, Colin. Marilyn will survive. She's tougher than you think.'

But the life of the studio, which normally made me feel so excited and important, seemed unbearably tedious now. I could hardly wait for the day to end. At five o'clock I rang Roger again, but he made it clear that I was not allowed to come over to Parkside House that night.

'Sorry, no can do. No visitors allowed. She's gone into hibernation. Maria's left two trays of food outside her room, but she hasn't touched them. Milton and Paula have both had long conversations with her keyhole, but the door stays locked. But she's in there, all right. I've just been up to check, and I think I can hear her snoring.'

'I'm getting worried, Roger. You said she was so well yesterday. Maybe she's ill. Maybe she's dying in there. Shouldn't you call a doctor?'

'I'm not in charge, Colin. Milton thinks she's OK. Evidently she's done this before, and she doesn't like her bedroom door being broken down by the fire brigade. Milton says let her sleep, so that's what I do.'

'But Roger . . .'

'Don't fret, Colin. I'll go up and check again this evening, I promise.'

Olivier was not at all sympathetic when I went to his dressing room after filming stopped.

'She's the stupidest, most self-indulgent little tart I've ever come across. What the hell's she playing at now? Tony says you took her out for the day on Saturday. What went wrong? Why can't she turn up for work? I don't want the

details. I don't care if you made love all afternoon. I just
want to know one thing: can you get her to come to the
studio tomorrow morning? Is she going to finish this film
or not?'

'Marilyn and I had a lovely, innocent day in the country,'
I said. 'But as soon as we got back, Paula got hold of her
and frightened the life out of her, and then Marilyn took
those pills. It was her way of re-exerting her control. I suppose Milton and Paula felt I'd threatened their influence.
Now they won't let me near her, or even talk to her. I doubt
if she'll be in tomorrow, but I can tell you one thing for
certain: she is determined to finish the film. She told me
so very seriously. In fact that was the only thing she said
about her work the whole day. Otherwise she just decided
to take a day off . . .'

'With you,' said Olivier grumpily.

'. . . and I happened to be around for her to take it with.'

'Well, if you should happen to "be around" again, try
to persuade her to come to work. She wants to be thought
of as a professional actress. She'll never be that, of course,
but if she turned up at the studio at all it would be a start.'

Dinner with Tony and Anne that evening was even more
sombre than before. Olivier had obviously told Tony not
to be angry with me, but I'm sure he felt I had let the side
down. The trouble was that, as usual, Tony did not really
understand what was going on.

When I went upstairs to bed, Roger still hadn't telephoned, and I didn't dare call him from the phone in the
hall, with Tony glowering at me and Anne listening to every
word. I must have finally nodded off, because when I heard

the scrunching of tyres on the gravel outside the house, my clock said 1.30. Then I heard Milton's voice calling from the garden.

'Colin!' He was standing on the lawn waving a torch. 'Colin!'

I opened the window as quietly as I could. Tony was a heavy sleeper, but Anne was not.

'What's the matter?'

'It's Marilyn.'

Life seems more dramatic in the middle of the night.

'Is she dead?'

'No, for heaven's sake, but she's not well. She said she wanted to see you right away. Get your clothes on and come down. She may be in a coma.'

There seemed to be a contradiction in there somewhere.

'What can I do?'

'I don't know,' said Milton, 'but it's worth a try. Otherwise I'll have to call a doctor. Hurry up!'

A doctor! That sounded bad. I pulled on a pair of trousers and a sweater, and crept down to the hall. I didn't dare to turn on a light, and in my haste I had several near-fatal accidents on the slippery oak stairs. What Tony would say if he caught me I did not even dare imagine. Outside, Milton was waiting in his car with the lights off.

'Get in,' he said. 'There's not a moment to lose.'

'No fear. I'm not being trapped at Parkside again,' I said. 'I'll follow you in my car.'

When we got to Parkside House, there was the same little huddle of people in night clothes and blankets which I remembered from air-raids in the war. Paula was clucking like a hen, Hedda was wild-eyed, and Roger very grave.

'I think we should break down the door,' said Roger, clearly fearing the worst.

'Not yet, not yet,' said Milton peevishly. A new door would cost a lot of money, and breaking in on Marilyn might upset her even more. Hovering in the background I could see Maria. She'll give notice tomorrow morning, I thought, especially if we break down the door.

'Colin should go up straight away,' said Paula. 'After all, she asked for him by name.'

'That was an hour ago,' said Roger grimly, 'and we've heard nothing since.'

'She's probably just sound asleep,' I said, 'and I doubt very much if she wants me to wake her up. But if it's the only way to get you all back to bed, I suppose I'll have to try.'

We trooped upstairs onto the landing, into the same corridor where I had first encountered Marilyn sitting on the floor – what a long time ago that seemed – and up to the bedroom door.

Tap. Tap. Tap.

'Marilyn? It's me. Are you awake?'

Silence.

Tap. Tap. Tap.

'Marilyn. Wake up!' The trouble was that I couldn't think of a reason why she should. 'It's Colin. I've come to see if you're all right.'

Silence.

'I think we should break it down.' Poor Roger seemed out of his depth. He was hoping this was 'a police matter', so he could take charge.

'It's two in the morning,' I said. 'Wouldn't Marilyn normally be asleep at this hour?'

'She slept all day,' said Paula.

What nobody dared say, but everyone thought, was that perhaps Marilyn had taken one too many pills.

'Let's go back down to the hall,' I said. 'Please, all of you just wait here until I say so. Roger, come outside with me, and bring a torch.'

They were so tired by this time that they did what they were told.

'I saw a long ladder in the garage, Roger,' I said. 'It's quite warm tonight, so the bedroom window will probably be open. I'm going to climb up and take a look inside before we do anything drastic.'

We found the ladder, and Roger pointed out which window was Marilyn's. It was slightly open, as I had guessed.

'As soon as I'm inside, you take the ladder away – I don't want Marilyn to know how I got in. She must think that her door wasn't properly locked, or I'll be out of a job. As it is I'm taking a terrible risk simply to calm down all those old women.' (He didn't seem to realise that that included him.) 'Then you go back to Marilyn's bedroom door – alone, please – and wait, in silence, until I open it from the inside. The others have got to wait down in the hall. I won't let the whole crowd barge in and disturb her. Especially not Milton. He might give her another pill.'

Roger held the ladder while I climbed up, carefully lifted the wide sash window and scrambled in. 'Go!' I whispered to him once I was safely inside, and shut the window behind me.

Like all great beauties, Lady Moore, the owner of the house, had installed blackout curtains an inch thick, and the bedroom was in total darkness. It took quite a bit of fumbling before I found the right cord and let in the moonlight. It took a full minute for my eyes to adjust enough for me to make out the silhouette of the enormous double bed against the far wall. I could also see three doors, although which one concealed Roger, and which went to a bathroom or dressing room, I could not remember.

'Marilyn,' I whispered. 'It's Colin.' I didn't want her to wake up and think she was about to be raped by some mad fan (or by me, for that matter).

'Marilyn, it's me. Wake up.' I approached the bed, stumbled over something, and sat down heavily on the corner of the mattress.

Now I could hear steady breathing, which was a huge relief, and I could also smell that wonderful warm, moist scent which beautiful ladies give off when they sleep. I put out a hand and patted the bed. Sure enough, the last pat hit skin. Marilyn seemed to be lying on her tummy across the width of the bed.

'Mmm . . .' I heard.

'I'm so sorry,' I said. 'It's Colin. I just wanted to make sure you're OK.'

'Hi, Colin. I thought you'd come. Get in.'

'Marilyn, everyone in the house is very worried. You wouldn't answer your door, and they thought you might be ill.'

'Oh, phooey,' said Marilyn, with a sleepy chuckle. 'Get in.'

'Wait,' I said.

I got up and went to door number one. It opened, so that wasn't the one. The next one was the same. The third door was locked tight, but there was no key. 'Roger,' I hissed through the keyhole. 'Are you out there?'

'What's going on? Is Miss Monroe all right? Why don't you open the door?'

'I can't find the key. Marilyn's fine. She's just asleep.'

'How do you know? Maybe she's passed out. Turn on the light. Better let me in.'

You must be joking.

'There's no key,' I said again. 'Marilyn woke up long enough to say "Hello." She's absolutely fine. Tell everyone to go to bed and leave her alone. They mustn't come back until they're called. I'll stay in here until morning. I can sleep on the sofa. Marilyn asked me to stay, so I'll stay. I'm not leaving her at the mercy of that lot in the hall. Now off you go, Roger. See you at breakfast.'

Roger snorted. He was meant to protect Marilyn, after all.

'Off you go, Roger, and goodnight.'

By the time I got back to the bed Marilyn was unconscious again, and this time my gentle pat could not rouse her. I sat down on the bed, and suddenly I felt very tired. What on earth was I doing there? I certainly could not take advantage of a sleeping Marilyn Monroe; but half of that huge bed was empty, and my eyelids were beginning to droop. If I could first take a little nap, perhaps I could work out what was best. Slowly, cautiously, I leaned forward onto the satin sheets, and fell absolutely fast asleep.

'Oh! Colin! What are you doing here?'

I woke slowly, to find myself lying face down on a very soft and sweet-smelling eiderdown quilt which I could not identify. 'What am I doing where?' I rolled my head around and stared. Marilyn was hunched up in the far corner of the bed, wrapped in the same pink coverlet which I had seen in the corridor, and lit by a small lamp on the table beside her.

'Colin? It's the middle of the night, isn't it? How did you get in here? I thought I locked the door.'

She didn't look scared but she did look a bit frantic, and I expect I did too.

'Oh, Miss Monroe,' I said (frown from Marilyn). I flailed around in the quilt in an effort to sit up on what was a dangerously soft mattress. 'Oh, Marilyn, I'm so sorry to disturb you. You see, Milton and Paula and Roger were worried that you might be ill. You weren't answering when they called.' I couldn't say that they thought she might have taken too many pills. 'And they said that they heard you call my name . . .'

'I must have been dreaming, I guess,' said Marilyn coyly.

'So they came and asked me to help, and I got in through the window,' I added lamely.

'The window?' Marilyn looked baffled. 'The window? Is there a balcony? Hey, it's like Shakespeare, isn't it? What's the name of that play? *Romeo and Juliet*. How romantic. But I'm not sick. What made them think that?'

'I haven't the faintest idea, Marilyn. If you ask me, I think they fuss over you far too much. You always seem fine to me.'

Marilyn gave a little smile and slowly closed her eyes, as if she were waiting for something.

'It's time for me to leave,' I thought, but that presented a problem. The only door to the outside world was firmly locked. I couldn't just slip away, and I did not feel it would be polite to start crashing around looking for the key as if I were trying to escape. How on earth had I got myself into this crazy situation? I was trapped in the bedroom of the most beautiful woman in the world, and there was nothing I could do. I cursed my stupidity in allowing myself to be fooled by all those panicky film people. But Marilyn was not asleep.

'I am fine, Colin, especially when I'm with you. I do see a lot of doctors, though.' Her voice was dreamy, almost as if she was talking to herself. 'Mostly sort of psychoanalysts, I guess. They're always telling me to explore my past.'

'Your past, Marilyn? Did you have a very terrible childhood?'

Marilyn gazed at the ceiling, and her great big eyes seemed to be unable to focus.

'Not terrible, Colin. Nobody beat me like they did you. It was just that nobody seemed to stay around for long. You know what I mean?'

'I don't believe in exploring the past too much, Marilyn.'

The bed seemed too wide for such an intimate conversation. I leaned towards her and came perilously close to doing a somersault. 'I believe in exploring the future. What is going to happen next? That's the important thing, isn't it?'

'You mean between us?'

'Oh, no, Marilyn.' I leaned back quickly. 'I didn't mean ... I mean ... I meant ... in the future.'

There was another long pause.

Now Marilyn leaned towards me. 'Do you love me, Colin?'

How is it that beautiful women can throw me completely off balance just when I think I am being smooth and wise and completely in control? Every time Marilyn looked me straight in the eyes I seemed to lose my grip on reality. I was certainly at the mercy of a powerful emotion, but was it love? And what sort of love? Love, passion? Love, sex? Love, romance? Love, marriage? I didn't know what language we were talking.

'Yes, I love you, Marilyn,' I said desperately, 'but I love you like I love the wind, or the waves, or the earth under my feet, or the sun coming out from behind a cloud. I wouldn't know how to love you as a person. If I loved you as a person, then I would want to possess you. But that would be impossible. I could never even dream of possessing you. Perhaps no man can, or should even try. You are like a beautiful force of nature, Marilyn, for ever out of reach.'

'But Colin, I don't want to be out of reach. I want to be touched. I want to be hugged. I want to feel strong arms around me. I want to be loved like an ordinary girl, in an ordinary bed. What's wrong with that?'

'There's nothing wrong, Marilyn. It's just not the way things are. You are a goddess to millions and millions of people. Like an ancient Greek goddess, you can come down to earth every now and then, but you always remain out of reach to human men.'

'I'm not Greek,' said Marilyn, clearly confused.

'Don't be upset. A goddess is a wonderful, glorious thing to be. It means that you are one of the most special beings in the whole world, and whatever those awful teachers and psychoanalysts say, you have achieved that all by yourself. You should be incredibly proud.'

Marilyn sighed.

'A whole film crew is dependent on your slightest whim. Great actors and actresses are waiting for your cue. Thousands of fans all over the world are laughing when you laugh and crying when you cry. Of course it's a very big responsibility. Of course you feel a tremendous lot of pressure. All goddesses do. But there is nothing that you can do to change what you are.'

Marilyn giggled, and edged closer across the bed.

'Sometimes I feel like a little child lost in a storm. Where can I hide?'

'You're not lost in a storm, Marilyn. You *are* the storm! You must never look for somewhere to hide. A good goddess crashes around making everyone else wonder where they can hide.'

'Oh, Colin, you are funny.' Marilyn began to smile again at last. 'But I'm a person, too.'

'Of course you are, Marilyn,' I said gently. 'You are a very lovely person. And you've got Mr Miller to take care of that very lovely person. Every goddess should have a dashing and handsome god to take care of her and remind her that she is also a woman. Any minute now he will be roaring out of the clouds to claim you, and he won't be a bit amused to find the court jester in his place. He'll probably throw a thunderbolt at me.'

'I won't let him hurt you.'

I couldn't help grimacing.

'Yes you will, Marilyn; and you'll hurt me too. But it will have been worth it.'

Marilyn sighed again and closed her eyes. Suddenly she looked very tired. I knew very well that I should tiptoe away and leave her to go back to sleep, but I seemed to have lost the use of my legs. I could only sit and gaze at this beautiful creature who seemed so innocent and yet wielded so much power.

'Colin,' she whispered, 'I have to tell you something. There is a part of me that is very ugly. Something which comes from being so ambitious, I guess. Something to do with all the things I've done – not bad things, but selfish things. I've slept with too many men, that's for sure. And I've been unfaithful so often I couldn't remember. Somehow sex didn't seem that important when I was a kid. But now I want people to respect me and to be faithful to me, and they never are. I want to find someone to love me – ugliness and beauty and all. But people only see the glamour and fall in love with that, and then when they see the ugly side they run away. That's what Arthur has done now. Before he left for Paris he wrote a note saying that he was disappointed in me. I saw it on his desk. I think he meant for me to see it. And then you came along and we had such fun and now I'm all confused. Why is life so complicated, Colin? Arthur says I don't think enough, but it seems I'm only happy when I don't think.'

'I'm sorry,' I said, 'but I'm not going to say "Poor Marilyn." You have talents and advantages most people only dream about. You just don't have anyone to help you use them properly. Like all ambitious people, you need to grow all the time – grow as an actress, and grow as a person too. And growing is painful, no doubt about it. Growing pains, they are called. But you don't want to stand still. You can't bear to sit back and think, "I'm Marilyn Monroe, and it's enough to go from one brainless Hollywood movie to the next." If you could do that, you wouldn't be here now. You wouldn't have married a famous writer, or read *The Brothers Karamazov*, or agreed to act with Laurence Olivier. You'd be driving a pink Cadillac in Beverly Hills, and having lunch with your agent every day, and counting the money in the bank.'

Marilyn opened her eyes. 'What makes me always want more, Colin? Do you think I'm being too greedy? Perhaps it's because when I was young I never had enough.' She sighed again.

'I never really knew my mom and dad. I was brought up in other people's homes mostly, but I did have a sort of auntie called Grace, who took care of me sometimes, and she was always telling me that I could be a great actress. "Norma Jean," she'd say, "one day you are going to be as famous as Jean Harlow," and she'd take me to the beauty parlour and get them to do my hair real nice. And she worked in movies too, so I always believed her.

'At one of the schools I went to, the other kids all called me "the mouse", 'cos I was so dowdy. My hair was brown then, too. I still feel like a mouse sometimes, running around in a film star's body. But then my bosom began to grow and I dyed my hair blonde. Some guy took my picture, and all the boys began to make a big fuss and try to make out with me. I didn't know any better, I guess. I used to have a lot of terrible pain every month – I still do – and I thought it was God punishing me for knowing about sex so young.

'I got married when I was sixteen. Poor Jimmie. He didn't really want to get married at all. He did it for a favour. Otherwise I would have had to go back to the orphanage. Grace couldn't take care of me any longer, you see. And I didn't know who I really was yet. I thought if I got married I'd be someone. I'd look after my husband and my house and I'd be someone.

'But it didn't work out like that at all. After a few months, Jim hardly came home at night, and when he did we had nothing to talk about. Then he went off to the war and I began to work as a model. Most marriages seem to break up in the end, don't they, Colin? Mine just fell apart. And I was unfaithful pretty often, I guess. Somehow it seemed natural to sleep with the photographer. I always did. Like giving them a reward for taking beautiful pictures. But modelling was fun. It was putting on an act. I always tried my very best, and I did good. When Jimmie came back he couldn't stand it. We got a divorce in Las Vegas about the same time as my first movie test. That was great. I just loved going in front of the movie cameras. Somehow it felt just right. But, boy, what a lot of men there are in the film business – and they all think you've got to sleep with them.'

'And did you, Marilyn?'

'Quite a lot. Too many. I didn't feel bad at the time. I was only a dumb kid. But I feel bad now. I feel guilty now.'

'I understand, Marilyn. But you mustn't feel guilty for the past. Everyone understands what it's like. I'm sure Arthur understands.'

'Joe didn't understand. He didn't like it at all. He married me, but I don't think he ever forgave me for what I did before I met him. That's not fair, is it?'

'Joe DiMaggio, you mean?'

'Yeah. He was great in so many ways. So strong. So sure of himself. I really tried to be a good wife to him, but by that time my work was starting to get better than his, and he had been so famous and all, and he couldn't stand that either. He got so jealous of everything. I guess I couldn't just change in the way he wanted me to. Then Arthur came along, and he was different. Arthur was always different from all the rest. Why, he wouldn't even sleep with me on the first date. He treated me like I was a real person. He was so wise. He didn't speak much – well, nor did Joe – but somehow you knew how smart he was just from looking at him. And he was so sexy. I really fell in love with Arthur, and I still am. But now I feel I've let him down. I must have, or he wouldn't have run away, would he Colin?'

'You and Arthur are hardly the typical honeymoon couple, you know,' I said. 'You are under incredible pressure to give a great performance in a very difficult film. You have to put all your efforts into your work, whether you like it or not. You've got Milton and Paula pestering you morning, noon and night. I don't expect Arthur had any idea what you would both have to go through. Right now he's running away from the whole bloody showbiz circus, not from you.'

Marilyn was looking so miserable that I couldn't resist stretching out my hand and holding hers. She didn't seem to notice for a moment, and then, suddenly, she gripped it with all her strength.

'Do you think so, Colin? Do you really think so?'

'Of course I do. In fact, I know that's what it is. He told Olivier that the pressure this film created was driving him crazy. He didn't say that *you* were driving him crazy.'

'But I saw the note on his desk. It said I wasn't the angel he'd thought I was. It made out that he was disappointed in me.'

'If Arthur really thought he was marrying an angel, he must have been nuts. Did he want a fantasy, or did he want a real person? He knew that you were the most famous film star in the world. Did he think you'd gone straight to where you were from heaven? Of course not. As you say, Arthur is a writer. Those notes he writes are just an author scribbling down random thoughts as they come to him. I've seen the way he looks at you. He understands you. He's proud of you. He adores you. It's just that he had no idea – no one has any idea – how much work is involved in making a film like this.'

Marilyn's voice was only just above a whisper. 'You don't think he's going to leave me, then? You think he'll come back?'

'I'm sure of it. And now it's time I left and you went back to sleep.'

'Oh, don't go away, Colin. I can't stand it if you go too.'

Marilyn opened up her swimming-pool eyes again and held onto my hand as if her life depended on it.

'Please stay, Colin.'

'All right, I'll stay. On one condition – that you come into the studio on time tomorrow morning. That will surprise everybody. That will show them all what you're made of. That will show them that you are a great, great star. That when things look bad you can rise above it and give the performance of your life.'

'Oh, Colin. You make it all sound fun.'

'Will you do it, Marilyn? Just once? Not for me – for yourself. We won't warn Paula or Milton or anyone. We'll just go. I'll set the alarm for seven o'clock. That gives us another four hours of sleep.'

Marilyn giggled. 'Four hours! Aren't we going to make love, Colin? Will that give us enough time?'

'Oh, Marilyn, you are a naughty girl,' I said sternly. 'We are not going to make love, OK? It's bad enough me being here. You've got to be able to tell your husband that we didn't even think about sex – that it never even crossed your mind. You've got to be able to say that with your hand on your heart. Otherwise he jolly well will leave you for ever. And you don't want that.'

Marilyn sighed. 'I guess so,' she said.

I gave her hand a squeeze. 'Just out of interest, though, would you have liked to make love?'

'Kinda.'

'Me too. But now we're going to sleep.'

'I tell you what, we'll spoon.'

'Spoon?'

'Yeah, I used to do this with Johnny – Johnny Hyde – when he was sick. Pull off your trousers and get into the

bed, Colin. Now lie very straight, with your face towards
the edge. Hey, it's good that you're thin like Johnny.'

Marilyn turned off the light and lay down behind me. I
could feel her stretching out her face towards the back of
my neck, until her body ran the whole length of mine. This
is getting dangerous, I thought. One thing could lead to
another in the dark. But Marilyn was clearly enjoying herself, being in control.

'Now slowly bring your knees up, Colin, and curl your
back forwards.'

As I did so I could feel Marilyn doing the same, until I
was completely enveloped in a soft embrace.

'See?' said Marilyn. 'Like a spoon!'

I breathed out at last. 'Goodnight,' I said. 'Sleep well.'

'Mmm,' said Marilyn. 'This is great. I will.'

Tuesday, 18 September

For the first two minutes, I was feeling so wonderful that I could not even imagine falling asleep. The next thing I knew, an alarm clock was going off on the other side of the bed, and sunlight was streaming into the room. To my amazement I could hear singing and splashing coming from the bathroom.

> 'I found a dream, I laid in your arms the whole
>   night through,
> I'm yours, no matter what others may say or
>   do . . .'

Marilyn was rehearsing the beautiful little waltz written by Richard Addinsell for the film – 'The Sleeping Prince Waltz'. So she can get up in the morning after all, I thought, if she wants to.

Then, as I clambered over the quilt to silence the clock, it dawned on me that I could be in serious trouble. I had just spent the night in bed with someone else's wife, and there were five witnesses right here in the house. I retrieved my grey flannel trousers from the floor and went into the dressing room. At least there was a sofa in there, even though it was rather short. I went back into the bedroom for a couple of pillows and that fancy pink coverlet and arranged them in careful disarray, to make it look as if I had spent the night as far away from Marilyn as possible. Only Maria would see it, I thought, so I must make sure she would notice. I might need her to give evidence later – I was not sure to whom. I put an ashtray and a glass on the floor by the sofa, as well as a pile of books.

'Marilyn,' I called. 'I'm going to the studio. See you there soon. OK?'

Marilyn came out of the bathroom in her white towelling robe.

'Hey, Colin, you look a bit messed up. What will Sir Laurence say? I slept great. I'm really going to show him what I can do today. Wait a minute, you need the key to escape.'

She laughed and went to her dressing table.

'There you are. Tell Roger I'll be down in ten minutes. See you later.'

It was already a quarter to seven.

' 'Bye, Marilyn. You are a star.'

I tore downstairs, almost crashing into Roger in the hall.

'Miss Monroe will be leaving in ten minutes,' I gasped.

Roger looked grim.

'Don't worry, Roger. She's feeling great.'

'I'll bet she is.'

'Now, Roger, don't jump to conclusions. I slept in the dressing room. See you at the studio. And please, put on a cheerful face. We can't have her losing her nerve now.'

'Morning, Evans,' I called cheerily as I roared off down the drive.

I managed to get to the studios just one minute before Sir Laurence's brown Bentley came round the corner of the dressing-room wing.

'Morning, boy! Is make-up ready?'

'I'll check, Sir Laurence.'

Olivier stopped and stared.

'You look a bit rough this morning. Anything up?'

'Everything is fine, I think, Sir Laurence.'

'Good. Well, let me know when Marilyn arrives. That is, if she does arrive at all. Any clues?'

'Oh, I think she will arrive this morning.'

Olivier gave me a piercing look.

'I really hope so,' I said to myself. You could never be absolutely sure with Marilyn.

'High time, too.'

He went into his dressing room and shut the door, while I went in search of the make-up man. Ten minutes later, to my huge relief, Marilyn's car appeared, Evans impassive at the wheel. Out got Roger. Out got Paula, out got Marilyn.

'Good morning, Colin.'

'Good morning, Miss Monroe. It's a lovely day.' I couldn't resist a grin.

'Yes, isn't it Colin!' and she grinned right at me, to Paula and Roger's obvious alarm.

'Make-up is waiting in your dressing room. I'll be back in an hour.'

'All right. See you then.'

I rushed along to Olivier's dressing room bursting with pride.

'Miss Monroe has arrived, Sir Laurence. She's being made up now.'

'What? At 7.15? Why, she's almost on time. What the hell brought that about? Colin, were you involved in this?'

Olivier glowered, and then gave a roar of laughter.

'You spent the night with her, didn't you? No wonder you look so scruffy. Oh dear, what will I tell K and Jane [my parents]?'

'Nothing improper happened, Larry, I promise.'

'I don't care if it did. At least you got her to the studio on time. That's all that matters. Now, let's settle down and try to make a film. And well done – but if I were you I'd go along to wardrobe and try to smarten up. And maybe to make-up too. And have a shower. You don't want the whole studio to know.'

Gradually the rest of the crew arrived, and one by one they nearly fainted with surprise. 'Marilyn!' 'Here already?' 'I can't believe it!' 'That's a first!' etc. The set was dressed and the lights rehung in half the normal time. David Orton kept me busier than usual on the studio floor, and I forgot all about Marilyn until her dresser came to find me two hours later.

'Miss Monroe would like a word, Colin.'

David groaned. 'At least let me know if she's ready, will you?'

'Oh, she's ready, Mr Orton,' said the dresser. 'She just wants a word with Colin first.'

'Oh she does, does she? Has Colin taken on Paula's job

too, then?' He raised his eyes to heaven. 'Lord, what did I do to deserve an assistant director like this?'

When I got to Marilyn's dressing room, she was still in the inner sanctum, but fully dressed and looking radiant.

'Colin, I'm feeling a little nervous now,' she said. She gripped my fingers hard. 'What do you think?'

'Marilyn, darling,' I didn't care if Paula could hear or not. 'Think of the future. You *are* the future. Now, come on the set and show those old fogies what you can do.'

It was a wonderful day. I only had eyes for Marilyn, although I didn't speak to her again. To my great relief most of the crew simply ignored me. It was as if my new role made me someone else, and put me on a different level. Paula fussed around as usual, but Marilyn seemed to have risen above her in some way, like a swan gliding through the reeds. She remembered her lines, came in on cue, and smiled brightly at the other actors on the set. When Olivier went over to give her some direction, she looked directly into his eyes and said, 'Gee! Sure!' instead of turning to Paula halfway through.

It was not until she was back in her dressing room at the end of the day that I got a chance to spend a moment with her alone.

'You were magnificent! You did it! You showed them all!'

'I was scared. Will you come by again this evening? Please? Come after supper. I've got to spend some time with Paula. I've got to learn my lines.'

The ice beneath my feet was wafer-thin, but I could not resist those eyes.

'All right. I'll come. But I've got no excuse to spend the night this time.'

'See you later then, Colin.'

'Goodbye.'

Tony and Anne looked pretty stunned when I reappeared at Runnymede House that evening. By now they knew where I had been the night before, and I don't think they ever expected to see me again. It was as if they thought Marilyn had swallowed me up, like a snake. Anne seemed rather upset, but Tony was full of congratulations.

'I don't know how you did it, Colin, but Laurence' – Tony is the only man in the world who calls Olivier 'Laurence' – 'was absolutely delighted. At this rate we'll finish the film early. What did you do? Do you think it will last?'

'I wouldn't bet on it,' I said.

'I think we can all guess what Colin did,' said Anne tartly. 'The question is, what happens next? And what will Mr Miller say when he gets back?'

'Marilyn and I are not having an affair,' I said wearily.

'No, of course not,' said Tony bluffly. 'Just good friends, right? Anyway, you're much too young for her.'

'And much too naïve,' added Anne.

'So you'll be staying here tonight, I assume,' said Anne.

'Ah, well, I suppose, I'm not sure about that. I have to drop by Parkside after dinner, just to make sure Marilyn is all right. She absolutely insisted. But I do want to come back here to sleep – if I can.'

'Quite,' said Anne.

When I arrived at Marilyn's house again Roger was pacing up and down outside, obviously waiting to talk to me before I went in. I parked as discreetly as possible and he came across, knocking his pipe out on his shoe.

'Miss Monroe is quite upset. She's with Paula at the moment. I'd leave them to it and wait, if I was you.'

'For heaven's sake, what's the matter now?' Colin, the twenty-four-hour cure! 'She was super today. Olivier was happy, she looked happy. It was as if the sun had come out.'

'You didn't think they'd let you take her over, did you?'

'I don't want to take her over. She's not a company. She's a person. I just want to help.'

'I think you'll find she *is* a company. Marilyn Monroe Productions. That's who pays my wages, anyway. And Milton Greene was here for an hour, too. He's plotting something, that's for sure. But I don't think he'll tell Mr Miller. I think he sees Mr Miller as a bigger threat than you.'

'So he jolly well should. Mr Miller is her husband. I'm nothing more than a passing fancy. Everybody in the movie industry fusses too much about what is happening that actual minute. Nobody takes the long view. It's a wonder any film ever gets finished at all.'

'It'll certainly be a miracle if we ever finish this one.'

Roger and I went into the kitchen to wait. Poor girl, I thought. I bet Paula is confusing her all over again. But then, I suppose that if she didn't, she'd be out of a job, just like the rest of them.

It was nearly dark by the time Paula appeared.

'Hello, Colin. You'd better go up. But don't stay too long. She's very tired, and she's not feeling too well.'

When I got up to the bedroom, Marilyn was lying down in the half darkness, looking very fragile indeed.

'Oh, Colin. I'm feeling so bad.'

'What has upset you now?'

'Paula told me that Sir Laurence yelled at her that I couldn't act, and never would be a real actress. And in front of the crew. The whole film crew.'

'Today? Olivier did that today? But I was there all the time.'

I was totally incredulous. I couldn't believe Olivier would do such a thing, especially today.

'No, I guess it wasn't today,' admitted Marilyn. 'Maybe yesterday.'

Oh, that Paula really was a witch. What an unkind thing to say!

'Well, I don't believe it, Marilyn. Maybe Olivier lost his temper and Paula got it wrong.'

'You think I can act, don't you, Colin?'

I sat down heavily on the side of the bed. Here we go again. How insecure can one person be?

'No, I don't think you can act! Not in the sense Olivier means. And thank God you can't. I'm fed up with Olivier implying that there is only one way to act – and that's his way, of course. Olivier can give great performances, but most of the time he's doing nothing more than dazzling impersonations, brilliant caricatures. He's a great stage actor. He can reach out across the footlights and hypnotise an audience into believing anything he wants. He loves to use tricks, false noses and funny wigs. He knows his craft backwards, and he carefully plans how to shock, and to seduce, and to beguile. But as soon as he has to be an ordinary person, he's dreadful. It's as if he needs some special exaggeration – a dagger, a hunchback, a false eye – in order to exist. Without them, he looks awkward and self-conscious. In his early films he was embarrassing.'

'I saw Vivien Leigh in *Gone with the Wind*,' said Marilyn. 'She was great.'

'She was great, Marilyn, because she wasn't impersonating Scarlett O'Hara in the film, she *was* Scarlett O'Hara. She knew exactly how Scarlett O'Hara would have felt. She got right inside the part. Olivier can't imagine that. He can put on a character and take it off like a suit of clothes, without any effort at all. That works fine for the stage, but you can't get away with it on film. The movie camera shows up everything. A great movie actor or actress has to *be* the part, right down into their mind. And that is what you can do, Marilyn. I don't know how, but you can do it. You are going to steal this picture away from Olivier, and he knows it. Mind you, he is a great man, and in one way I don't think he minds. I really admire him for that. He can see what you've got – I don't care what Paula says – and he's prepared to hand you the film on a plate if that will make it a success. He wouldn't do that unless he knew, deep down, that you were an actress. It's the same with Marlon Brando. Olivier admires him, but he also fears him. The problem is that neither of you acts the way he acts, and that is very hard for him to understand. And he can probably see that you are the future, which must frighten him a bit.'

'Oh, Colin. What should I do?'

'Get to the studio as early as you can, dear Marilyn. No one expects you to behave like a bit-part player, but the film can only be finished if everyone turns up. There are some lovely music sequences coming along, and you enjoy those. And there are some nice scenes where Elsie Marina takes control of the love affair, and those will suit you very well. In fact, I want you to take control of the film. Marilyn Monroe Productions and Laurence Olivier Productions – you're equal partners, aren't you? It's time you put your foot down. Forget about poor little Milton; he's just a stooge. Forget about Paula; she's only there to hold your hand, and she's scared stiff of you anyway. Even forget about Mr Miller. He can't take the heat. You'll have plenty of time to make him a good Jewish wife when you're back in the Bronx. You've got to march into that studio and take control. Lay it on the line: "This is the way I want it, and this is the way it is going to be done."'

'Gee, Colin, do you think I could? But I'm too scared. I'm scared that when I get in front of that camera I won't feel right – that I won't know what to do. I wish I had a few of those tricks of Sir Laurence's up my sleeve.'

'God forbid, Marilyn. Do you want to be a ham like Bette Davis? Of course not! You always know exactly what to do when you're in front of the camera. You are a natural. An incredible natural talent. Don't be scared. Enjoy it. Revel in it.'

'There you go again – you make it sound fun. Why do I get such bad nerves?'

'Listen, Marilyn. When I left school I went into the air force and became a pilot. I was flying single-seater jet planes every day. When I was in the plane, I was sitting so far forward that I couldn't even see the wings. And sometimes I would look out into the vast blue sky and think, "Help! What's keeping me up? Nothing but thin air. Any minute now I'm going to fall twenty thousand feet into the sea." Of course I knew all about aerodynamics and that stuff, but for a moment I would panic and my heart would stop. But then I would think, "It's not for me to worry about that. All I have to do is fly the damn plane. And that I can do, or I wouldn't be up here on my own in the first place." Then I would be back in control again; and as you can see, the plane never fell.'

Marilyn clapped her hands. 'You're right. I'm going to fly! I can fly! But first I've got to be free. Free of all those pills and doctors. Free of everyone.'

'And free of me.'

'Oh, Colin, no. Stay a little while. Lie down beside me till I fall asleep. Please. I feel I can't be alone tonight. Otherwise I'll have to take the pills. And anyway, I want you to tell me all that stuff again – about being natural, I mean. That's what I really want to be.'

'All right, Marilyn. I'll stay a little while, but for now, let's get some sleep.'

I turned the light off and lay down in that soft quilt again and closed my eyes.

I heard Marilyn giggle in the dark.

'Natural. Do you think you and I could ever be natural together, one day?'

'Perhaps, Marilyn. When the film is over, perhaps. It would be nice.'

'Mmm,' said Marilyn. She reached out, took my hand and held it. 'Natural is nice . . .'

Less than an hour later, she was awake again.

'Colin! Colin!' she cried.

I sat bolt upright in the darkness and fumbled desperately for the light. I had fallen asleep on top of the bed and, thank goodness, fully dressed. I had not even taken off my shoes.

'It hurts. It hurts.'

Marilyn lay on her back, clutching her stomach. She was as pale as a ghost.

'What's the matter?' I reached out and put my hand against her cheek. She didn't seem to have a fever. 'What's the matter?'

'It's cramp. I've got cramps. It's terrible. Oh no! Oh no! Oh no!'

'What is it, Marilyn?'

'The baby! I'm going to lose the baby.'

'The baby? What baby? Are you having a baby?' I simply could not comprehend what was going on.

For the first time since I had known her, Marilyn began to weep. I had never seen so much as the sign of a tear in the studio, even when Olivier was at his worst. I suppose I thought of her as someone whose life had been such a struggle, who had known so much pain as a child, that she would never allow herself to cry again.

'Poor Marilyn,' I said, as gently as I could. 'Tell me about the baby.'

'It was Arthur's,' Marilyn said, between sobs. 'It was for him. He didn't know. It was going to be a surprise. Then he would see that I could be a real wife, and a real mother.'

A mother – I could hardly believe it.

'How long have you been pregnant?'

'Just a few weeks, I guess. At least, my period is a couple of weeks late. And I didn't dare mention it to anyone, in case it wasn't true. Ow!' Another spasm gripped Marilyn's tummy. She was clearly in terrible pain.

'I'm going to lose the baby. Maybe it's a punishment because I've been having such a good time.'

'Nonsense, Marilyn. We didn't do anything wrong. Nothing at all. I'd better tell Roger to call a doctor right away. And he'd better tell Milton too – only you are not to take any pills. Shall I get Paula and Hedda too?'

'Don't tell them about the baby, Colin. I always have cramps when my period is due. They're used to that. This seems just much worse, that's all.'

'OK. But you'd better tell the doctor about it when he comes. I'll be right back.'

'Please come back soon, Colin. Please don't leave me alone.'

I rushed out of the room and down the corridor to Roger's bedroom, and turned on the light.

'Roger! Wake up at once. It's Miss Monroe. She's ill.'

'What's the trouble?' Roger was out of bed in a flash, and pulling on his trousers and shirt.

'You'd better call a doctor at once. She's not seriously ill, but she's in a lot of pain. The telephone operator will know the name of a local doctor who's on call at night. Try to find someone who'll come right now. Then, and only then, can you wake Paula and Hedda and send them along.

And call Milton too, I suppose. In the meantime I'll be holding Marilyn's hand.'

Roger shot off downstairs to the telephone and I went back to the bedroom. Marilyn was nowhere to be seen, but there was a light under the bathroom door.

'Are you OK, Marilyn?' I called. 'Roger is talking to a doctor right now. He'll be here very soon.'

Marilyn let out a cry. 'Ooh! I'm bleeding so much.'

'Listen carefully, Marilyn, this is important. Don't lock the bathroom door. If it's already locked, as soon as you can, reach out and unlock it. Even if you have to crawl on your hands and knees. I promise I won't come in. I won't let anyone in. But you might faint, and the doctor has to be able to get in as soon as he comes.

'Oh, Colin!'

I heard a shuffling noise and some groans, and then a click as the bolt was pulled back.

'Good girl.'

Roger appeared at the bedroom door.

'The doctor's on his way. I'm going to call Paula and then Milton. Let me know if there's anything I can do.'

'Hang in there, Marilyn,' I called out. 'The doctor's on his way. Try to take it easy if you can.'

'It's not the pain, it's the baby. I should have stayed in bed for a few weeks.'

'Marilyn, if it's not to be, this time round, it's not to be. You and Arthur are just beginning. You'll have plenty of time after the film is finished. Don't upset yourself too much. What will be, will be.'

At that moment Paula hurled herself into the room, and

I had to jump in front of the bathroom door to stop her from bursting in.

'Marilyn! Marilyn! My baby! What has Colin done to you?'

'Colin's done nothing, Paula,' said Marilyn through the door. 'Don't be silly. I'm just having a very bad period, that's all.'

Paula glared at me.

'We've done nothing wrong at all,' I said firmly. 'Trust me, Paula. No one is to blame. Poor Marilyn isn't ill. It's her monthly cramps, that's all. The doctor is coming just in case.'

Paula slumped down beside me on the carpet, ever the tragedienne.

'Marilyn, Marilyn. What can I do? Why isn't Arthur here? He should be by your side. Colin is a nice boy, but he isn't your husband. Oh dear, oh dear, you'll have to cancel the film now.' She sounded exactly like a typical Jewish mum.

Roger was the next person to appear at the bedroom door. 'I've telephoned Milton,' he said. 'He's on his way too. Soon we'll have the whole bloody circus here. I'll go down and wait for the doctor.'

It was not long before we heard a car drive up outside.

'The doctor's here,' I called through the door.

But it wasn't. It was Milton.

'What in God's name is going on, Colin? What have you two been up to? Where's Marilyn? Why isn't the doctor here yet? You should have called him before you called me.'

'Marilyn's in the bathroom, and she does not want anyone to go in. Repeat, *not*,' I said severely, looking at Paula, who had stood up. 'No one is to go near her until the doctor arrives. I promised Marilyn I'd personally bar the door.'

There were occasional groans coming from the other side, and Milton and Paula were both desperate to investigate further, but mercifully, at that moment another car could be heard, and soon Roger appeared with an amiable-looking elderly man.

'Now then, where is the patient? What on earth are you all doing here?'

'The patient is Miss Monroe you see, and . . .' gabbled Milton and Paula at once.

'The patient is in the bathroom here,' I said loudly. 'And all of us are now going downstairs.' I started shepherding them out like a lot of bleating sheep. 'My name is Colin Clark, doctor,' I said over my shoulder. 'The bathroom door is unlocked. We will leave Miss Monroe to you.'

And we left.

'This is Dr Connell,' I heard him say as I closed the door. 'May I come in?'

Downstairs in the hall Milton and Paula looked at each other, and me, with equal hostility.

'This is absolutely nothing to do with me,' I said. 'I was simply waiting for Marilyn to fall asleep before I went home. She'd been complaining of stomach cramps, and didn't want to be left alone. Then she said she was feeling worse, so I told Roger to call a doctor.'

There didn't seem anything else to say, so no one spoke. Soon, to my relief, we were joined by a sleepy Hedda Rosten.

Hedda sometimes to get tipsy in the evenings, but she is a nice, motherly lady, and is not part of the film world. If anyone could help to calm down Marilyn, it would be Hedda.

There was an uncomfortable fifteen minutes of foot-shuffling and hand-wringing before the doctor came downstairs.

'Is Miss Monroe's husband here? No? Well, which of you is in charge?'

We all stepped forward.

The doctor raised his eyebrows. It was very late at night.

'Well, Miss Monroe is in no danger. I've given her an injection and the bleeding has stopped, and she is going to sleep. I suggest that you ladies' – he frowned at Milton and me – 'take it in turns to stay with her. She should stay in bed tomorrow for the whole day, but after that she should be fine. I'll come back to see her at lunchtime.'

There was a huge sigh of relief from us all. Paula and Hedda went upstairs immediately to inspect their charge and decide who slept where. I suspect Paula wanted to ensure that she was the first person Marilyn saw when she awoke.

'Let me walk you out to your car, doctor,' I said.

'Me too,' said Milton, anxious not to leave me alone with anyone, ever again.

'You weren't surprised to find that your patient was Miss Marilyn Monroe, doctor?' I asked as we got out into the fresh night air.

'Oh, no, Mr Clark. My wife is the head of the Sadler's Wells Ballet, so I'm used to leading ladies.'

'The head of the Sadler's Wells Ballet? I must know her then. My father is on the board of the Opera House. What's your wife's name?'

'Oh, no,' Milton groaned. 'Here we go again. Isn't there anyone you don't know, Colin?'

'She is called Ninette de Valois,' said the doctor.

'Oh, how lovely! Of course I know Ninette. I admire her enormously. What a coincidence. Do give her my love. Tell her from one of the Clark twins.'

'I will. And what are you doing here, Mr Clark, if I may ask, in Miss Monroe's house at two o'clock in the morning?'

'I'm working on the film Miss Monroe is making at Pinewood Studios, and I'm, er, a friend of Miss Monroe's as well.'

'And Miss Monroe's husband? I presume she has a husband?'

'He's in America. I think.'

'Oh, really? And how long has he been gone?'

'Oh, a week. Six days, to be exact. And the baby, doctor?'

Milton looked completely stunned.

'Oh, you know about that, do you? Well, it's true. Miss Monroe was about three weeks pregnant, I would say. Not now, of course. But she can always try again. It isn't the end of the world. I must be off. Goodnight, gentlemen.'

And he climbed into his car and drove away.

'I'd better be going too,' I said.

'Yes, Colin, you had. I told you it would end in tears.'

'My conscience is clear, Milton.' I said. 'No tears from me. I'm sad for Marilyn, of course, although I find it hard to think of her as a mum.'

'Perhaps, Colin . . .'

'I'll tell you what, Milton. I'm going to see Marilyn once more, tomorrow. Just once, I promise. After that I'll vanish back into the scenery. OK, Milton? Goodnight.'

The fairy story had ended, as dramatically as it had begun.

Wed`nesday, 19 September

'Marilyn, darling, the time has come to say goodbye.'

As I drove over to Parkside House the next day I knew
exactly what I had to say. Somehow I had an image of
Marilyn, reclining on a garden bench in the shade of a
beech tree, wrapped in her white towelling robe. I would
walk across the lawn towards her. She would be very pale,
lying there with her eyes closed, very quiet but not asleep.

'Marilyn, darling . . .' I rehearsed it again. One thing
was certain: she must wipe our friendship from her mind
completely. I had telephoned Milton from the studio at
eight a.m., and he had told me that Arthur Miller was
returning that very afternoon, five days earlier than
planned. He had heard of last night's happenings from
Hedda, I suppose, and while I did not think she would have
mentioned me, there was a very real danger that Marilyn
might, just to make him jealous. Added to this, she could
sometimes be mischievous. 'I kissed Colin,' she had said to
Milton, just to tease him, and she had thought it highly
amusing, although Milton – and I – had not. Milton had
warned me that if Marilyn ever became dependent on any-

one, she tended to add them to her retinue without too much thought of the consequences. She thought nothing of having two psychoanalysts, two dramatic coaches, or two Hollywood agents at the same time. She had sometimes had two lovers simultaneously in the past, as Milton himself could testify. It wasn't that she was duplicitous or cunning. It was simply that she really didn't think it was important. She seemed incapable of comprehending the effect she had on those who surrounded her, and how much she meant to them; this even applied to her husbands, I suspect.

I had made sure that I was at the studios earlier than usual, and that I was waiting outside the dressing rooms when Olivier arrived.

'Morning, boy.' Olivier's usual greeting. 'Marilyn here yet? Is she going to surprise us again?'

'I'm afraid not, Sir Laurence. She was taken seriously ill in the middle of the night. Well, it looked serious, anyway. A doctor had to be called, and he said she must stay in bed all day.'

'Good gracious. Bed all day? That sounds bad. And what illness did the doctor diagnose?'

'It turns out that it's only a very bad period. But Marilyn was in considerable pain, and she lost a lot of blood.'

I wasn't going to mention the baby. That was something private between Marilyn and Arthur.

'I see. Josh Logan warned me about that possibility. Evidently she always needs a day off once a month. We allowed for that in the schedule. But of course we've used up all that time by now. Whatever next?'

'Milton tells me that Arthur is returning from New York

this afternoon. I'm sure that will help. Marilyn told me she's going to work especially hard every day from now on, like she did yesterday, and I think she's serious. Her relationship with Arthur was a bit frantic when they first arrived, and his departure gave her a terrible shock. I think she'll concentrate on her career for a while now. At least until this film is finished.'

'I hope you're right, Colin.'

'And it's time I got out of the equation, Larry. So with your permission I'll go over to Parkside this morning and make that clear. Not that there has been anything improper between Marilyn and me, but I wouldn't want Arthur to misunderstand.'

'No, quite so. You run along. Try to find out if she'll be in tomorrow. Please assure her that we all want to finish this film as soon as possible. Personally I wish I'd never set eyes on the woman, but don't tell her that.'

What a pity it is that Olivier never let himself get to know Marilyn properly, I thought, as I drove to Parkside House. This could have been a great film, and a wonderful experience for all of us.

Marilyn was awake, Roger told me when I arrived, and the house was full of people as usual. She was in the bedroom – so much for my shaded lawn – and I did not have the courage to go in unannounced. It was nearly an hour before Paula took pity on me, and called me upstairs.

'Marilyn, it's Colin. Do you want to see him?'

That was bad. I hadn't needed an introduction yesterday.

'Sure. Oh, hi, Colin. Come on in. Now, don't say you've come to say goodbye.'

How did she read my mind so accurately? You could never tell with Marilyn.

'You're not going anywhere, are you? I've decided I want to finish the film as quickly as possible. Why, it was you who told me I must do that. And Paula is going back to the States soon to get a new permit or something, so I'll need you to hold my hand as well as Sir Laurence.'

'I'm sorry, Marilyn,' I said, taking no notice of Paula, who had sat down beside me, 'but I don't think you should even catch my eye after today, let alone hold my hand. Mr Miller is coming back this afternoon, and it's so important that he doesn't find out that we're friends, or have been friends over this past week. We both know that we did nothing wrong. We know that we just had fun and enjoyed each other's company. But Mr Miller might find that very hard to understand. He might think that while the cat was away, the mice were behaving like rats.'

Marilyn gave a weak laugh.

'I guess you're right, Colin. He never seemed to mind about that sort of thing in the old days, but he's much more intense now.'

'Marilyn, darling, you are his wife now. And I don't care what you say about the note you read on his desk – he worships you. Just as I do.'

Marilyn sighed.

'The trouble is that you never can believe how wonderful you are,' I said. 'I suppose it's because of your childhood. You assume that everything nice is going to be taken away from you in the end, so you're frightened to get your hopes up.'

'I adore Arthur, too,' said Marilyn in a whisper. 'I really do. He's so strong, and so wise. And he's a gentleman. He always treated me like a lady. I wanted to marry him from when I first saw him in Hollywood, all those years ago . . .' She paused.

'I think you're made for each other,' I lied. 'You need someone who takes you seriously. Who sees what a great person you are. No ordinary man could do that.'

Marilyn looked relieved. 'Gee, Colin. You make me feel better right away.'

'You are great, Marilyn. And you are going to have a great career, and a great life. Mind you, after this production is over you must be more careful which films you decide to make. Maybe you should take Mr Strasberg's advice. Not about your day-to-day routine, but about scripts. He knows a lot about scripts.'

Paula beamed, suddenly my ally for life. She got up and went to the door. 'I'll leave you with Colin now,' she said.

'When this picture is over,' Marilyn went on, 'I'm going to settle down and be a good wife to Arthur. I'm going to learn to make matzo-ball soup just as good as his dad's. I'm not going to make any other movies until I've shown Arthur I can look after him. He'll never want to leave me again, that's for sure.'

'So you see why it's so important that he shouldn't suspect that there was anything between us?'

'Nothing serious. He wouldn't think that, would he? That would be terrible.'

'Well, he might. So you must be very careful. You must say nothing at all.'

'Nothing?'

'Nothing. Just imagine what his reaction would be if he thought that I'd done something which had resulted in you losing his baby.'

Marilyn gasped.

'I'm sorry to be so blunt, Marilyn, and we both know that I didn't do any such thing. But just imagine. What would he say? What might he do? I know what would happen if our parts were reversed and you were my wife.'

Marilyn opened her eyes wide.

'I'd kill him.'

'Oh, Colin.' Marilyn began to sob quietly. 'I love Arthur so much. How can I show him? How can I convince him? Do you think I can ever give him a child? Do you think he wants a child? We've never discussed it. I know he'd be a wonderful father. Why, he's like a father to me. I'll never lose him. I'll make it all up to him. I'll never disappoint him again.'

'Of course you won't, Marilyn. And I don't think you ever have. He's frightened now, just as you are. You are both artists, great artists. Did you think it was going to be easy? Great artists need other artists in their lives. It takes one to understand one. But they will always clash – every now and then. A great writer like Mr Miller needs to be selfish in order to create his masterpiece. And so do you. Sure, an actor like Olivier can just walk out on the stage and play a part. But when you give a great performance, you actually *become* the person; you feel their joy and feel their pain. That is an incredible strain, but that is what makes you a star.'

'Ooh, Colin.'

Marilyn was beginning to cheer up. 'So what must I do now?'

'Give Arthur a great welcome home. No sex for a bit, though. Tell him how much you missed him. Tell him you've decided to settle down and finish the film as quickly as possible. Tell him that you won't bother him when he is writing – Milton said he had some deadline now. Ask him to come and pick you up at the studio each evening when Paula is away. Whenever Paula is here, don't let her stay with you past seven in the evening. All good, simple rules, Marilyn, and not too hard to obey.'

'Yes, sir,' said Marilyn, giving a little salute. 'Anything else?'

'Yes. Never look at me, not so much as a glance. You may be a great actress, but I'm not, and my face could easily betray what I feel.'

'What *do* you feel, Colin? Tell me.'

'I feel incredibly lucky to have been able to spend a few days in the company of the most wonderful, brave and beautiful person in the world, but . . .'

'"But"?'

'But if Arthur ever mentions my name, you've got to shrug and say, "Colin? Oh, he's just a messenger, nobody of any importance at all."'

'Oh, Colin. I couldn't say that. But I understand about Arthur.'

Marilyn stared gloomily at the quilt. Then suddenly she brightened up.

'I'll tell you what – I'll wink. No one can stop me winking

at you, and you've got to wink back. When things get tough at the studio, when Sir Laurence gets mad, I'm gonna look for Colin, and wink. And you'd better watch out. Paula is going back to New York soon, so I may wink quite a lot.'

It was such a brave, childlike solution to a potentially tragic situation that I lifted Marilyn's hand up off the bed and kissed it.

'I'll wink back,' I said. 'Never fear.'

POSTSCRIPT

And so it was over. A brief flirtation between a young man of twenty-three and a beautiful married woman, who was as innocent as she was mature.

No one really seemed any the worse. Marilyn had lost the baby, of course, but I am not sure that was such a bad thing. I simply could not imagine her as a mother. There had been nobody to look after her as a child, and consequently she had no idea how to look after anyone else. Each time she had got married she had tried desperately hard to take care of her husband, but she always made a total mess of it, and they ended up looking after her. She was, I am afraid to say, just too self-obsessed.

Marilyn always said that she had an ugly side to her character, but if she had, I can honestly say that I never saw it. Confused, frightened and totally lacking in self-confidence, she had not got that sense of her own identity which is so essential for a stable life. Like many celebrities she felt that she couldn't cope with the demands that were thrust on her, and this made her quick to suspect the motives of people whom she had allowed to get too close.

Luckily I never fell into that category, so we could remain chums.

Marilyn's idea that she had a dark side helped her to explain why everyone seemed to desert her in the end. She never knew whom she could trust, and this was because the answer was probably: 'No one, no one in the whole world' – all though her life.

One reason she failed to take people with her was that she had no idea of where she was going herself. Nevertheless, she got there. No one can dispute that, and, basically, she did it on her own.

Imagine how many blonde starlets were being abused by those horrible Hollywood moguls night after night – and still are, for all I know. They all faded away, but Marilyn did not. Nearly forty years after her death she is still the most famous film star in the world.

After our adventure, the filming went on as usual on the set of *The Prince and the Showgirl* at Pinewood. Marilyn became a little more punctual and, compared to her behaviour on her subsequent films, she was very professional. All the dubbing and 'post-sync' work, for instance, was completed in a couple of days, far quicker than anyone had imagined possible. Marilyn seemed to have resigned herself to finishing the movie first, and being the perfect wife to Arthur Miller later, although she never ceased to gaze at him with awe and to obey his slightest command.

She did sometimes wink at me in the studio, especially when it seemed that Laurence Olivier was about to explode. Because it could ease the tension, Olivier did not mind. Indeed, after filming had finished he took me with him into the theatre as his personal assistant. Two years later I was winking to his wife, Vivien Leigh, who had become just as unstable as Marilyn ever was, from the wings of the Burgtheater in Vienna. Perhaps I was born to wink.

After Marilyn went back to America, I never spoke to her again – but I did hear from her once, or at least I like to think so. In early 1961, a friend of mine in Olivier's office rang me in New York to say that Marilyn Monroe had telephoned the night before and left a number for me to call. He had not spoken to her himself, he said. He had just found a note on his desk. Of course, it could have been someone playing a joke. I was well known for supporting Marilyn, although this was increasingly hard to do as she became more and more unstable. The rest of Olivier's circle, including Olivier himself, actually welcomed reports of her deteriorating condition as evidence that their opinion of her had been right all along. It was only towards the end of his life that Olivier was able to relent.

When I got the message, I must admit that I hesitated. Apart from the possibility that it was a hoax, I was not sure that I could handle a distraught Marilyn on the line. She was famous for making long, rambling calls, and I knew that I would not be able to help her. It was clearly far too late to wink.

In the end, I did dial the number, and I could hear it ringing away in the Californian night. But no one replied, and I am ashamed to say that I was relieved. It was not that I had abandoned her, certainly not in my heart. It was just that by now nobody could help her.

Poor Marilyn. Time had run out.

Appendix

Letter written by Colin Clark to
Peter Pitt-Millward in Portugal,
26 November 1956

Dear Peter,

At last the filming is over and I am back in London
again. You can't imagine what a relief it is not to have to
get up at 6.15 a.m. and spend the day in a hot, crowded
film studio with a lot of quarrelsome prima donnas. It took
a total of eighteen weeks to make the movie, including two
weeks for preparation, and by the end we were all heartily
fed up. I thought of you every night, and not always too
tenderly either, because that was when I would write my
daily diary, or journal, as I promised you I would. The
trouble was that I was usually very tired, and I couldn't type,
or my clacking would have kept other people awake, so I
wrote it by hand. My handwriting got worse and worse until
finally it was virtually illegible, and the whole thing is a
mess. I might transcribe it one day, but I doubt it. Who on
earth would want to know the day-to-day details of how a
film is made? Nevertheless, it was a great experience to
work with Marilyn and Olivier. I don't think the final film
will be any better than my diary, but they are both 'wonderful people to know'. I am going on working with Olivier in

a few weeks' time – this time in the theatre – and although I will probably never see Marilyn again, I will certainly never forget her. Well, even you are one of her fans, and you've never seen any of her films.

The thing about Marilyn is that she is a mixture. She can be sweet and funny and innocent; she can be a tough and ambitious go-getter; she can be totally lacking in self-confidence; and she can do a pretty fair impression of Ophelia after Hamlet has gone. Since she is also an excellent actress in her own way – not like Olivier, of course, but I think she is *better* than him in this film – you will realise that she is a pretty hard lady to pin down.

Poor old Olivier did not appreciate this at all. All he saw was a Hollywood blonde who was always late, didn't learn her lines and refused to listen to his directions. I think that when he first met her, and agreed to do the film, he thought he could have an affair with her. But after a few weeks on the set, he would gladly have strangled her with his bare hands. Marilyn is more astute than she looks, and she was well aware of how Olivier and his hand-picked English crew felt about her. She had her own supporters whom she brought from the USA – her partner Milton Greene, Lee and Paula Strasberg, a secretary called Hedda, and her new husband, Arthur Miller. They certainly were not the team I would have picked ... They are all Jewish – as are her lawyer, her agent and her publicity men – while Marilyn is a typical California blonde; so how they can understand the way her mind works, goodness knows.

No wonder the poor woman often looks so confused!

When Marilyn first arrived, I wasn't much bothered

about her. After all, I know Vivien Leigh pretty well, and Marilyn had stolen Vivien's part in the film and all my loyalty was to the Oliviers. But I found myself being seduced by Marilyn's image; her aura is very powerful indeed. Gradually, just working on the film wasn't enough. I was determined to get to know her more directly – although, given that as third assistant director I was the most unimportant person on the whole production, that looked very unlikely. However, it was not impossible. When I was working in the office it was me who had hired Marilyn's servants, and her bodyguard (ex-Scotland Yard), and rented the house she was living in, so one evening I invented an excuse and went over there to try my luck. Imagine my surprise when I did meet the great star – but not at all in the circumstances which I expected. I was so absolutely stunned that I stopped writing my diary for a whole week, and when I started again I changed the dates in case anyone got their hands on it. I seriously thought that I might be sued or bumped off. It is hard to imagine, but there is so much money riding on Miss Monroe's pretty blonde head that people get very, very ruthless.

What actually happened was that after a few drinks with Roger (the ex-cop) I went out for a pee and stumbled right into Marilyn, sitting on the floor in a dark corridor outside her bedroom door. Whether she had had a row with Arthur Miller or not I don't know. She simply stared at me and said nothing, so I backtracked as fast as I could and hoped I'd got away with it. If she had made a stink about it the following day, I would certainly have been fired. That she did not do, but it turned out that she *had* remembered, and after filming she called me into her dressing room and asked me if I was a spy. Luckily I could absolutely swear that I was not, and I must say that I felt jolly sorry for her, too. She hasn't got many (any?) real friends, and Miller had told her that he was going away to Paris and New York for the following ten days. And they are meant to be on their honeymoon. I was so grateful to Marilyn that she hadn't said a word to anyone about my foolish escapade that I swore my undying loyalty there and then – which was a little rash, since Laurence Olivier is my boss.

I did not tell anyone what had happened, and I thought that was the end of it, but the next day Marilyn actually telephoned me in Olivier's dressing room. She had not been in to work as she was seeing Miller off, and she asked me to go via her house again on the way home. I assumed she had more messages for Olivier or something. She found it very hard to talk to him directly by that time. Even so, I didn't tell Olivier where I was going, in case he thought I was plotting something behind his back. Then, when I did get to the house, Marilyn asked me to stay for supper, and I could see that she was just lonely and wanted someone to chat to. I am six years younger than her, and I suppose I was one of the few people around who wasn't trying to get something from her.

Anyway, we were getting along famously when Miller – yes, I know, he's her husband – had to ring from Paris. Marilyn immediately looked hunched and defensive, and I left toot sweet.

Marilyn did not come in to the studio the next day – Olivier had given her a day off – but everyone seemed to know I had had supper with her. Olivier thought it was frightfully funny. He absolutely takes my loyalty for granted, and so he should. Milton Greene, as Marilyn's partner, had a complete fit. To make matters worse, Marilyn had told Miller I was there when he rang – to make him jealous, I suppose – and the upshot was that I was forbidden ever to talk to Marilyn again, on pain of death. Sad, I thought, but what's a boy to do! However, as I was soon to learn, you can't get involved with Marilyn without getting involved with Marilyn. The following day was Saturday. I was staying with a very kind couple called Tony and Anne Bushell, who are great friends of Olivier. Tony is Associate Director on the movie, and as such does not approve of Marilyn at all. Just before lunch, Roger, the cop, turned up in his old car and announced that he had come to take me out. As we drove away, Marilyn jumped out from under a rug on the back seat, nearly giving me a heart attack, to say nothing of Tony Bushell. She was bored of her stuffy house, she said, and she wanted an adventure.

So I took her to Windsor Castle and we saw my godfather, Owen Morshead, who is librarian there. He gave us the grand tour, which Marilyn seemed to enjoy, and then we went and had a look at Eton. It was a glorious sunny day, and Marilyn could not have been jollier or more natural, but I felt rather apprehensive nonetheless. After all, she is the most famous film star in the world. Once she did demonstrate her power. 'Shall I be "*her*", Colin?' she asked as we left Windsor Castle, and she gave her famous wiggle. Immediately she was recognised, and a crowd began to gather, until we had to get into the car and flee.

When we got home, Marilyn's lawyer was waiting for me, full of dire threats, but Marilyn rose to her full height and told him that if he lifted a little finger against me it would be him who got fired, not me. Even so, I kept my head down on Sunday. Everyone was talking as if Marilyn and I were having an affair, which was jolly flattering but complete nonsense. Milton Greene came over and gave me a long lecture about the dangers of getting involved – he seems to think Marilyn Monroe is *his property* – and I agreed to stop. Monday was just a normal day at the studio. Marilyn did not appear, and I thought it was all over.

But in the middle of the night, there was little Milton again, outside my bedroom window. Would I get dressed and go back to Marilyn's house at once? She had locked herself in her room and did not respond to anyone. 'Why should she?' I thought, but I suppose I was flattered to be asked to help. I went over and joined the little group of sheep bleating outside her door, but to no avail. Finally, I had an idea. I went outside to the garage with Roger-the-cop and found a ladder. I put this against the wall under Marilyn's window and climbed up and in. All I meant to do was open her bedroom door from the inside so that her female companions could get in and check on her health. I could hear her sleeping, so at least she was alive. But she had taken the key out of the lock, so I couldn't get out without waking her up and being caught *in flagrante*. I went back to the window but Roger and the ladder had gone, so there was nothing to do but take a nap and wait until dawn, when I could find the key and escape. An hour later, however, Marilyn woke up. There's no doubt she was pretty

startled at first, especially as she clearly remembered lock-
ing the door. I managed to calm her down, and then she
suddenly decided that it was like *Romeo and Juliet* – me
coming in by the balcony – and was very sweet and kind.
She said she did not want to be left alone, so I spent the
rest of the night there (No – I behaved impeccably) and I
persuaded her to come in really early to the studio the next
day. This she did, which went down very well with Olivier
and the crew, and I was a bit of a hero.

On the next night, I had decided that I better not sleep
there again, but then Marilyn really did feel ill, so I said
I'd stay until she fell asleep – she has a lot of trouble sleeping and often takes pills, like you – and then she got terrible
cramps, and I had to wake the whole house up and call a
doctor. (Can you imagine, he turned out to be the husband
of Ninette de Valois, the head of the Sadler's Wells Ballet,
who I know quite well. What a coincidence.) It seemed that
Marilyn was not in any danger, so I fled. I mean, after two
nights, people might have easily got the wrong impression
and thought that I'd done something to make Marilyn ill.
And it is not as if Marilyn was just a little wardrobe girl or
something. Apart from anything else, she is MARRIED, and
sure enough Arthur Miller came scurrying back from New
York the next day, four days earlier than planned. I had to
keep my head down as much as I possibly could for the
next week, and go back to being the little messenger boy
whom everyone could shout at. But what an adventure it
had been.

I've told you all this in lieu of the diary, because if it had
been in the diary it would have been the best bit, if you see

what I mean. It probably looks like a lot of crazy nonsense to someone so far away, but please keep it until I come out next time so that I can take it back and put it with the journal, however scruffy that is. I might want to write it all properly one day.

As ever,
Colin

INDEX